TEAM ON THE RUN

MAINSTREAM *SPORT*

TEAM ON THE RUN

THE INSIDE STORY OF THE LINDA McCARTNEY PRO CYCLING TEAM

JOHN DEERING
FOREWORD BY SEAN YATES

MAINSTREAM
PUBLISHING
EDINBURGH AND LONDON

First published in Great Britain in 2002 by
MAINSTREAM PUBLISHING COMPANY (EDINBURGH) LTD
7 Albany Street
Edinburgh EH1 3UG

ISBN 1 84018 782 4

This edition, 2003

A catalogue record for this book is available from the British Library

Typeset in Garamond and Gill
Printed and bound in Great Britain by
Cox & Wyman Ltd

This book is dedicated to the Kitchen of Love

Contents

Foreword by Sean Yates

Reading John's book brought it all back, all the mixed emotions, all the frustration, all the sadness and also all the good times. It seems it happened a long time ago, another lifetime.

Yes, we all move on, and soon forget what happened in the past. But John has done a great job of telling us the brief history of the Linda McCartney Pro Cycling Team. After finishing my Pro career in '96 I did not really have a clue about what I was going to do for the rest of my working life. I have never been one for thinking too much about what lies ahead. So when I had the opportunity to get the Linda McCartney team up and on the road I just thought, 'OK, this is what I must have to do next.'

It turned out to be a great experience, although it could have been a lot better. Would I do it again knowing the outcome? Difficult question. I prefer to just remember the good times, and the great people I worked with. Although I do have one definite thought: personally there is no way I feel Julian Clark can be excused for what he did to so many people, no matter how great the good times were.

So read on, and get an insight into what went on in that brief moment in time.

Yours in sport,
Sean Yates

Introduction

Hello. I'm John Deering. I'm not very famous, so I'd better tell you who I am before we get started.

I was 30 when the Linda McCartney team started, 31 when I joined, and I've just turned 35. It doesn't sound like a long time, but it's long enough for virtually everything to have changed in my life in between.

I used to work at Sigma Sport in Kingston-Upon-Thames, selling bikes, and now I do again, so that's one thing that hasn't changed, I suppose. I've got a band called Dipper. At the start of the story I've got a wife, Louise, and we've got a dog, Kit. I think that's all you really need to know about me. I'm a cycling fan, of course.

This is the story of the Linda McCartney Pro Cycling Team, but somebody else's version of it might read differently. This is my personal viewpoint of events as I saw them, as they happened to me and around me. By necessity, some of the things I talk about are based on hearsay and conjecture – I can't be sure of all the facts, just how things appeared at the time, or how we've all tried to make sense of them since.

The McCartney days will possibly always be the best of my life. I don't regret one minute of what happened, nor do I hold any disregard or dislike for any of the fantastic people I was with at that time. They were a good bunch.

It's a good story – I hope you agree.

John Deering
July 2002

Acknowledgements

Thanks firstly to the scholarly Martin Booth for keeping me pointing in the right direction and for his professional encouragement throughout the writing of this story. Britain's No.1 cycling facts man, Peter Lambert, was on hand to point out my numerous mistakes.

Matt Illingworth, Matt Stephens, Chris Lillywhite, Spencer Smith, Louise Deering and Ben Brooks all reminded me of some of the high and low points of our time on the tarmac, whilst also filling me in on some of the gaps. Jason Turner and Ian Whittingham were good enough to support me throughout when I should have been working for them at Sigma Sport.

My Mum and Dad gave up their dining-room for an office . . . no small gesture in a household that enjoys its food so much.

Thanks most of all to the big feller himself, Sean Yates, the only man I know who lives on a diet of water, olive oil and sugar. Yes, we know, Sean: there's no fat in sugar, right?

Chapter 1: The Lovely Linda

There's a certain kind of heat that you only seem to get in the Southern Hemisphere, where the air itself seems on the verge of catching alight. On the particular afternoon I have in mind, it was pushing 40 degrees in Adelaide city centre. As the multi-coloured swathe of cyclists pummelled their pedals up the long, straight drag through the centre of the Adelaide Parklands, they shimmered in a silver glare that was hard to look at directly. Stuart O'Grady was happy; he'd just picked up a two-second time bonus that would give him the overall victory in the 2001 Tour Down Under. The 100,000 or so South Australians leaning over the barriers around the circuit for the final stage were happy too, as O'Grady is one of their own.

David McKenzie of Linda McCartney wasn't so content. He'd watched a break of 20 or so riders go clear at the front of the race, and he wasn't in there. With none of O'Grady's main rivals involved, and O'Grady himself delighted to see any remaining time bonuses picked up by the move, Macca felt certain that this break would decide the stage.

'Who have we got in there?' he asked of Max Sciandri, his captain.

'I think we've got two guys,' replied the Anglo-Italian.

Weighing up his options, McKenzie took off in pursuit of the rapidly disappearing breakaway. Closing a gap down on your own is never an easy task: a group working together should always be stronger than one man alone, but within two 4.5 km laps Macca had bridged across to the escapees. Getting his breath back, he realised that Max had been wrong – he found himself the only McCartney man involved.

Feeling pretty good, and unsure of his chances in such a big group if it came down to a straight sprint for the line, he set about removing some of the opposition. First he upped the pace at the front, stretching the riders into a long thin line as each man struggled to maintain his position close to the wheel in front. Their lead over the following pack breached the three-minute mark with 35 km left to race. Other men in the group took it in turn to come alongside Macca to share the pacemaking, and he slid back into fifth or sixth place in the line, slipstreaming momentarily and gathering his strength.

Then he attacked, launching himself wide of the group and clear at the front, eventually creating a splinter group of nine, as the others, already tired from matching the high pace in the heat, faded away to be recaptured by the chasing bunch. A nine-man group significantly improved Macca's chances of victory, but the odds were still not to his satisfaction. With less than two laps remaining, he launched another attack that nobody could match. Those last two circuits went past in a blur for the man from Melbourne, his head down, sweat dripping onto his handlebars as he sucked every last drop of power out of his aching body to turn the biggest gear he dared. The effort was enough to give him a beautiful solo victory.

He sailed across the line to a reception reminiscent of his famous stage win in the previous spring's Giro d'Italia, arms aloft, proudly displaying his new green and gold strip and the logos of his new sponsors, Jacob's Creek and Jaguar. Their first race in harness with Linda McCartney, and already they were winners. The season stretched out in front of the new team: new riders, new races, new horizons. Yet it would all be as concrete as the heat mirages shimmering on the Adelaide tarmac on that January afternoon. Incredibly, that was the last time anybody rode a professional bike race in a Linda McCartney jersey.

'I remember the first time I met Julian Clark,' says Jason Turner of Sigma Sport. 'It must have been in the spring of 1998. He walked into the shop and said, "I'm Julian Clark of the Linda McCartney Pro

Cycling Team. Can I have some saddles? Our saddle supplier will replace them for you."'

Did he go away with his saddles?

'Yes, he did.'

And were they replaced?

'Yes,' recalls Jason, lifting an eyebrow in satisfaction at the memory, 'yes, they were. Eventually.'

Cycling is the second most popular sport in Europe. Its calendar is rich in history, common memory and nostalgia, images of hard men, faces etched with pain, toiling across Somme or Passchendaele landscapes, racing over the continent's highest mountain passes to fling themselves across a line drawn across a road somewhere in France, Italy, Belgium or Spain.

People remember cyclists with a reverence other sports find hard to match: Fausto Coppi, the Italian world-beater who won the biggest races on either side of the war, despite spending many of those dark days within a British prisoner of war camp, and then dying of malaria whilst still a young man; Eddy Merckx, 'The Cannibal', winner of any race he cared to take part in; Sean Kelly, hewn out of the barren Irish countryside his family had farmed for generations to become the world's best cyclist; Greg LeMond, returning to take his second and third Tour de France wins after being shot by his brother-in-law in a gory hunting accident; and another American, Lance Armstrong, beating certain death from testicular cancer and going on to become a multiple Tour winner.

Cycling fans can be a strange breed. They love their sport, and there are those amongst them who are rarely interested in anything else. When the Tour de France visited the UK in 1994, millions lined the streets of southern England for a chance to see their heroes. Football might be more popular among Joe Public, but not everybody who watches a game on the telly is passionate about the sport. It sometimes seems that every cycling fan is a devoted follower, to the exclusion of all other activities. When England played Greece at Old Trafford for a place at the 2002 World Cup, businesses across the country were deserted as the nation huddled around TV sets at home or thronged every pub . . . except bike shops. They did their normal brisk Saturday trade, interrupted only by the odd bemused, 'Oh, is there a game on?' from a punter if the proprietors had the temerity to switch their own tellies on for a look.

Against this backdrop, an English team once tried to make its way into the closeted world of European cycling. As the only British team of note for many years, its sponsors stood to reap the profits of 'owning' the sport in Britain. The papers might not talk about cycling too often, but if they did, it was impossible to do so without mentioning the team. And sponsoring a cycling team is not like sponsoring a football team – you get to 'own' the riders too. For instance, David Beckham plays for Manchester United, and he happens to have Vodafone written across his chest. If his team were a cycling team, they would be *called* Vodafone.

This is the story of the Linda McCartney Pro Cycling Team. It didn't last too long, but it was fun.

Julian Clark was an ideas man. A successful motocross rider since his teens, he had ridden at international races all around the world. By his 20s, he was running his own Kawasaki works team. Later, he would own a gym at Brands Hatch frequented by the great and good of British motorsport. But fame and fortune always seemed to go hand-in-hand with rack and ruin for the man with the vision, and by the Christmas of 1997, he was on his uppers, working 60 hours a week for cash in hand to support his young family after he had lost everything when the gym business collapsed.

Still fit, he rode a racing bike from job to job, working through the night and riding home in the small hours, keeping the whippet-thin physique that had seen him through his years on the motocross circuit and to the finish of a couple of triathlons that year. He had been out riding with his local cycling club, the 34 Nomads, where his enthusiasm and strength belied his novice's lack of knowledge about the sport, intriguing the regulars.

One day, out shopping with his wife Tracie, loading the trolley with some of the Linda McCartney vegetarian ready meals that were an ever-present in their freezer, he had a St-Paul-on-the-road-to-Damascus moment.

'I stood there with one hand on the trolley staring at this frozen lasagne,' he said. 'What a fantastic idea! What better advertisement could there be for this stuff than a sports team living the vegetarian lifestyle and eating this gear?'

That night was a long one for Julian and Tracie as they built a proposal for the Linda McCartney Pro Cycling Team. The team would be British, but would one day compete in the Tour de France. All the riders, management and staff would be vegetarian. They would prove beyond all reasonable doubt that the vegetarian lifestyle was a healthy way to live and a perfect platform for sporting success. And Linda McCartney would shift shed-loads of TV dinners as a result.

'The proposal seemed like an excellent one to us; but then we do get an awful lot of proposals,' said John Treharne. His company, Tim Treharne Consultancies, was headed up by his dad, and they were the prime link between the McCartney family and McVities, the manufacturers and distributors of Linda McCartney Foods. Tim had worked with Linda and Paul for many years. Linda held control of the content of the food, the packaging and the way it was marketed, and through Tim she was in close contact with McVities' Linda McCartney factory in Norfolk, where the meals were manufactured. 'We passed the proposal on to Linda and Paul, as we do with all the reasonable ones, fully expecting to get a "Thanks, but no thanks". It was a lovely surprise to get, "Great idea, let's go for it".'

Julian was given a small budget and carte blanche to run the team however he thought best. 'I knew absolutely nothing about cycling, I hadn't even ridden a proper bike race at that time,' he confessed. He made a few calls, helped by the guys at his cycling club who knew a few people. British cycling is a small world – if you know somebody, you probably know everybody. Within a few weeks, he'd put a tidy little team together. Mark Walsham was his star turn, a rapid-finishing home-based British pro approaching the end of his racing days, but nevertheless a recognisable face and still a force in UK racing. He also got Simon Cope, a stalwart of the local bike scene and something of a criterium specialist. Criteriums, or crits, are the races held on tight circuits, usually around a town centre, that had been a way of life for British cyclists through the '70s, '80s and early '90s. Through them, he found a skinny blond Yorkshireman called Rob Reynolds-Jones, Scott Gamble, a hard-working rider from Nottinghamshire, and Neil Hoban, another strong cyclist who had been doing the rounds of the smaller semi-pro teams.

The sixth member of the squad would be Julian himself; it sounded like an episode of *In at the Deep End*, where some chirpy TV presenter used to whistle a sheepdog into rounding up some rowdy ewes, or land an ailing 747 packed with dignitaries. For the old guard, it was all wrong. Cyclists are meant to be bred from birth, little men carved out of walnut who would think nothing of training for 20 hours a day on a glass of water, faces forced forever into a grim expression as they pass from one dour discipline to another: start with schoolboy track racing, do some cyclo-cross, a few crits in the evenings, a road race every weekend, miss out narrowly on selection for the Milk Race before finally reaching their zenith, the veterans' 50-mile time trial. You couldn't just rock up after 30 years of doing something else and expect to be good at it.

How annoying for all the others when he didn't make a fool of himself. He wasn't going to set the world alight, but he proved himself a useful teammate, an impressive (if less than stylish) climber, and a fierce competitor. Later that year he would take his best-yet placing in a Premier Calendar event, the Brian Rourke Grand Prix in Staffordshire, where he finished an admirable fourth.

The new team was shaping up nicely. Their aim for 1998 was to find a place in the newly inaugurated Prutour, the Tour of Britain. It was to be the biggest race the UK had seen for some time, featuring massive investment from Prudential, and attracting some of the world's best teams to come and race across the country for a week in May. Julian wangled his new team an entry, joining the other professional British team to be invited, the totally dominant Team Brite. The whole Linda McCartney set-up for their first season was focused on finding a place in the Prutour and garnering maximum publicity from a limited budget. It was no coincidence that they were a six-man squad and the Prutour was inviting six-man teams.

Julian had struck up a friendship with one of the 'daddies' of the south-west London bike scene, Chris Lillywhite. Chris was known to all and sundry in the bunch as 'Cel'. This was not, as some thought, a joining together of his initials, but an abbreviation of 'celery', a reference to his love of Chelsea FC, closely associated with the said root vegetable since the glory, glory days of the '80s. Did I say glory, glory? What I actually meant was disappointing, dreary, useless days of scuttling between the First and Second Divisions. The dashing of hopes is a feeling familiar to any Chelsea fan who can remember a time before Glenn Hoddle, and not entirely unknown even in the time of Jimmy Floyd Hasselbaink. 'Good training for life,' my Dad called it. I guess that was his way of coming to terms with all the pain and suffering he had caused his son by passing on the Chelsea gene. I blamed *his* dad, my grandad. He could have gone anywhere, could have gone to the Arsenal or somewhere useful like that, but he picked Chelsea and the curse rumbles on.

Cel was probably the most successful cyclist currently riding in Britain. It felt like he had been around forever, but he was actually only just past 30. He had turned pro much younger than usual in order to take advantage of the good money there was to be made in winning criteriums and road races in the mid-'80s. Now he was riding for the Harrods squad, and still racking up big wins in races like the Lincoln Grand Prix. There wasn't much he hadn't won over the years.

The year before his season with Harrods, things had been a bit thin on the ground for UK pro cycling. Cel had ridden as a lone professional for Sigma Sport, the shop in Kingston-Upon-Thames where I worked part time. I had a proper job too, flogging bits of computers, but Sigma was like a club where the great and good of the region would congregate. As a result, I got to know Julian and Cel. Cel and his wife Jane were both season ticket holders at Stamford Bridge, and as a result of his racing programme there would often be a spare. I got used to sitting in Row G of the Matthew Harding Upper under the name of C.J. Lillywhite and seeing my boys either delighting or withering depending on how they felt from week to week. Both Julian and Cel liked to join our merry band of bike-shop types for the occasional Kingston Monday or Friday jolly-up, so we got to know one another fairly well.

Both of them ended up going to the Tour of Slovenia as preparation for the Prutour. It was racing to a standard far above anything Julian had experienced before, and on the first day he was quickly struggling, through no fault of his own.

'I think that the Tour of Slovenia was my eighth race. Eighth race ever, that is,' remembered Julian. To put it in context, this would be a bit like having a couple of kickabouts for your school team before turning out for Man U. Or Brentford, at least.

The first stage is a rolling sweat under a 34-degree heat, and it wasn't long before our brave soldier pulled his back wheel on the first climb and was forced to receive mechanical attention. 'I hardly knew the front end from the back then, I didn't know what had gone wrong.'

'I jumped out of the car, and there was a motorcycle cameraman filming him,' remembers Topper Taylor, the mechanic. 'He wouldn't move out of the way for love nor money, and I nearly ended up in a fist fight with the twat, just to put Julian's wheel back in. By the time we'd got it sorted and looked up, the race had vanished. Not a living soul in sight.'

Julian set off up the road in pursuit of the race, hopeful of 'getting back in the cars', the race convoy vehicles aiding a rider's passage back up to the bunch. After about 20 minutes flat-out effort without seeing so much as an exhaust pipe, the panicking future-supremo finds himself at a T-junction.

'Go right son, right!' hollered his team manager, earthy northerner Dudley Heyton. Another 12 kilometres of frantic pedalling ensued, without any sight of the last car, before a terrible thing happened. Julian arrived at another T-junction. Except it *wasn't* another T-junction. It was the SAME T-junction.

'Right lad, get in t'cars,' advises Dudley.

By now apoplectic, the inexperienced rider shouts, 'What d'yer think I'm trying to 'kin do? I've been trying to get in the 'kin cars for the last 'kin hour!'

'Nay lad, I mean get in the car!'

'Oh, I see.'

There followed one of the more unusual sights in cycling, as Topper secured the bike on the roof and the three outlaws set off once more – now all seated in the manager's car.

'I hadn't been in that situation before, and I thought, "maybe this is what you do".' Julian's bewildered skinny figure sat in the front seat as Dudley conducted a conversation with a local rustic in his best Slovenian, and they hared off in what they now hoped was the right direction. After an incredible 40-minute drive – 'I don't remember much about the scenery' – they finally made visual contact with a race helicopter hovering over their long-lost friend, the *peloton*.

'Right lad, put your race cape on,' said the director.

'Dudley, it's 34 degrees outside,' reasoned the rider.

'Put your cape on, cover up your numbers, and don't cheek me again!' shouted Dudley.

Five minutes later, they're closing on the last car. 'When I get up to that farm track on the left, jump out and get pedalling, son,' instructs the creative Dudley. And so it came to pass that Julian Clark rejoined the field after the best part of two hours, and a passable rendition of *Trains, Planes and Automobiles*. Wearing a cape.

'Where the hell have you been?' asked an incredulous Chris Lillywhite, when the man who would one day be his teammate finally rode up beside him, sweating freely.

'Cel,' came the reply, 'if I told you, you wouldn't believe me.'

Slovenia was good, tough preparation for the Prutour, and the team were confident that they could be a useful little force at the race. However, their plans were thrown into disarray just a few days before the start, when Scott Gamble, their best rider of the early season, broke his wrist. That left the Linda McCartney squad with only five fit riders going into a race that demanded a team of six.

Going into the race a man short wasn't an option. Still, there were plenty of riders around the UK Premier Calendar circuit not attached to teams that had been selected . . . surely Julian would pick one of those chaps to make up the numbers? No. He was having one of his big ideas.

Julian still didn't really know many people in cycling, but he knew enough about Sean Yates to know that it would be a fantastic PR coup if he could tempt him out of retirement. Sean in his heyday was unarguably England's most popular cyclist. In a professional career lasting 15 hard seasons, Sean rode 17 major tours and countless classics, scoring many great victories along the way but largely dedicating his career to helping his various team leaders over the years. He was seen as the ultimate *superdomestique*, the man you would want at your side before all others. It was that loyalty and diligence that people seemed to like about him, and made him a cult hero to cycling fans in Britain and beyond. He was more of a water-carrier than a star, but a star among water-carriers.

Sean wore the yellow jersey of Tour de France leader, won the Grand Prix Eddy Merckx, stages in both the Tour de France and Vuelta a Espana, the National Road Race Championship, the US Pro Championship and the Tour of Belgium in his own right. Having established himself as one of the world's leading time triallists, Sean's win in the 1988 Tour de France long time trial set a record for the fastest stage in the race's long history.

He retired at the end of the 1996 season, moving back to Sussex satisfied with a job well done. He settled into an idyllic rustic routine that involved tending a few gardens for some pocket money, picking the kids up from school in the Land Rover and doing the odd time trial at the weekends. He went sailing with his brother Christian and rode his motorbike, and he and Pippa talked about moving to the Lot or

Dordogne in France, where they could bring up their two boys in rural simplicity. He sold the boat and the motorbike in preparation. Perhaps he was secretly bored.

When Julian called Sean, the start of the Prutour in Edinburgh was only a few days away. A season and a half had passed since Sean's last meaningful race action, but he couldn't stay away from the bike completely. Pippa told stories of how she would send Sean out to the garage for another bottle of red, or to fetch something out of the big chest freezer, only to hear the unmistakable whirr of his stationary turbo trainer being turned at an unbelievable rate for a minute or two. The big man would walk back into the kitchen carrying the bottle and wearing a sheen of fresh perspiration. His body shape had changed a little. He hadn't put on weight as such, but the shorter efforts of time trials and errand-running turbo-sessions had bulked his legs out, so he looked more like a track rider than he had in his lean racing mode. Those same legs were still shaved as they had been since . . . since . . . well, since they'd needed shaving for the first time. The varicose veins were, frankly, disgusting, but he wore them as battle scars.

The conversation with Julian went something along the lines of:

'Hello, I'm Julian Clark from the Linda McCartney team.'

'Hello.'

'Would you like to ride the Prutour next week?'

'No, not really.'

After his first instinct to refuse, Sean thought about it a bit more. Against riding: 18 months since his last road race, an hour a day on the turbo was hardly ideal preparation, a wedding to go to the day before the race ended, and he was supposed to have retired from all this sort of shit anyway. For riding: it was exciting, Julian would pay him £1,000, and it had to be better than gardening. He told Pippa about it, expecting her to tell him to grow up and act his age: he had just turned 38. To his surprise, she said, 'Yeah, do it. Why not?'

'I went up into the loft and got my old Motorola kit down,' he remembers. 'There was my bike bag, my kit bag, racing shoes, all that sort of thing. It was a very strange experience. I think I got that call on the Wednesday, and on the Friday I flew to Scotland for the start.'

The Prutour went pretty well for the fledgling squad. They were unable to win a stage or place anybody too high on the overall standings, but they contributed well to the racing and were always in the public eye. This was due in no small part to Sean being treated like Shackleton returning from the Antarctic wherever he went. People loved him.

Julian got into a split with Sean on the tough moorland stage that straddled the Lancashire heights before dropping down into Blackpool. 'There were quite a few guys in there; about 20-odd I think, all strung out in one long line,' remembered Julian. 'I was just gritting my teeth, hanging on to the wheel in front and hoping I wasn't going to get spat out the arse of the group. I heard somebody shout at me and looked to my right: there's Sean, coasting along next to me. "Come on, you need to be nearer the front if you're not going to get shelled out," he yelled, and told me to get on to his wheel. Nearly crying with the effort and the general unfairness of it all, I pulled out of the line into his shadow and he towed me all the way up the line to about three or four from the front. "Nobody's going to let us in up here," I was thinking to myself, as it seemed pretty bad form to just push in. Sean rode up alongside Jean-Cyril Robin, who was best French finisher in the Tour de France, I think, and murmured something to him in French. Unbelievably, Robin eased slightly for a second, leaving me a gap, and smiled to allow me in.'

Julian had seen at first-hand how much respect Sean still commanded in the *peloton*. 'I asked Sean later what he'd said to Robin. He said, "I told him you were paying my wages and if you got spat I'd be in the shit." Charming . . . but he was smiling.'

They roomed together during the race, Julian gleaning every little scrap of information about cycling that he possibly could from Sean. The night before the Pennine stage that took in the horrible climb of Rosedale Chimney, Julian was nervous about the following day's action. He asked Sean for advice on how to tackle the hill: he'd heard stories of top pros being caught out by how steep it was, having to get off and push, all sorts of humiliations. There was also a technical problem. The little team didn't have enough 25-sprocket cassettes to go round, and so he would be riding a 23 – would that be enough? (Incidentally, this already shows that Julian was learning about cycling. '23' refers to the number of teeth on the biggest cog on your back wheel – 25 is a lower gear than 23, so it's easier to get up super-steep climbs like Rosedale Chimney. At the other end of the chain, where the pedals and cranks are, there are two bigger rings, normally a 53 for most quick riding and a 39 for the climbs. Earlier that year, another cyclist, Matt Illingworth, had talked to Julian during a race and said, 'I was in the 53–17 all the way along there. What about you?' 'Err . . . fifth?' came the confused reply.)

'Don't worry about the Chimney,' Sean told Julian, 'there's a knack to it.' The boss sat up in bed, all ears. 'I remember going up there in the Kelloggs (the Prutour's predecessor) a few years ago. The toughest bit is the bend at the bottom. Boys who haven't been up there before get caught out, have to stop, and can't get started again. The trick is to put it in a big gear for the last bit before you get to the climb. Give it everything along there, and your speed will carry you round that bend.'

Armed with this essential bit of insider knowledge, Julian slept soundly. The following day saw our man flying towards the bottom of the climb in a huge gear, then beginning to struggle slightly as the road began to slope up. It got harder and harder, and they weren't even on the climb proper. All Julian could think about was how strong Sean must be if he could so easily carry such a big gear up to this fearsome bend, but he continued to follow the advice, fighting to turn the gear round as others overtook him in easier gear combinations. By the time he hit the steep bend at the bottom, he was virtually stationary, and had to quickly click down through all his gears until he was in plumb bottom, the 39–23. Even this was far from comfortable, and it was all he could do to stop from just clipping out of his pedals and collapsing at the side of the road. Somehow, he managed to keep his bike jerking forward, conquered the corner and struggled to the top, gasping for air.

That night, he professed his admiration for the man who had told him to keep a big gear rolling into the corner.

'I don't know how you do it, Sean. You must be some kind of monster if you can roll up quickly to the bottom of a climb like that.'

'Oh yeah, sorry about that,' said Sean. 'It wasn't the same climb as I was thinking of.'

If looks could kill!

By the Saturday of the race, the penultimate stage, Sean was packing up his old Motorola kitbag. As prearranged, he had a wedding to go to, and the race would finish without him. The cycling public smiled and scratched their collective head: was it a mirage? Did they really see Sean Yates riding the Tour of Britain, or did they dream it?

Sean and Julian struck up a good friendship during the 1998 Prutour. Julian told Sean about his plans for the team to grow, telling him that the vegetarian ethic was a big PR vote-winner and that he wanted to take the team to the Tour de France in the next few years. He wanted to know if Sean would be interested in becoming the manager, or DS (*directeur sportif*) in cycling terms. After the race, Julian had a big freezer delivered *chez* Yates, and began having the couple supplied with Linda McCartney frozen-food deliveries.

Sean was in a bit of a dilemma that summer. He went back to his garden rounds, with a spot of labouring for a local building firm here and there while he and Pippa planned their French move, but he now had two possible high-profile jobs open to him. A phone call from his old Motorola teammate Steve Bauer had thrown up an interesting possibility. Bauer had been approached by Lance Armstrong about becoming manager of his new American team, but Bauer wasn't interested. He thought, however, that it sounded right up Sean's street: why didn't he give Lance a bell?

Lance was back in business after losing two years, and very nearly his life, to cancer. He and Sean had been closer than close as teammates at the USA pro team, Motorola; Sean ended up doing about two years more than he had intended there to help the young Armstrong develop. Their boss at Motorola had been Jim Ochowicz, 'Och', who had been unable to find their set-up a new sponsor when Motorola pulled out at the end of the 1996 season. The French team Cofidis had snapped up Armstrong, who was going places, but had cynically turned their backs on him when the cancer was diagnosed. Now he was back, untried and untested, but with the backing of an American squad again, the United States Postal Services (USPS) team.

Sean rang Lance about the job. They'd kept in regular contact since Sean's retirement and right through Lance's illness and recuperation. Johnny Weltz, another contemporary of Sean's, was the DS at USPS, while the purse strings were controlled by Thomas Weisel, but the real boss was already Lance Armstrong: he decided who was hired and fired. He wanted to bring Sean in alongside Johnny and Sean was interested. USPS weren't massive yet, but they got in the big races and they were on the up. By the end of 1998 it would be clear that Lance was back in a big way and they would be a major force in 1999.

But Sean had some reservations. There were a lot of politics involved in the power struggle at US Postal. 'I don't think Lance got on too well with Johnny, and that concerned me a bit,' said Sean. 'Also, I should admit that I was a bit put out that Lance had called Steve Bauer before me, which made me think that I hadn't been first choice. That felt a bit awkward, because when Och was searching for a new sponsor to replace Motorola, the deal was that I would be his assistant DS and Lance was going to be the leader, so I suppose I was expecting Lance to back that arrangement.'

Meanwhile, Julian was pushing hard for Sean to say yes to Linda McCartney, and seemed a lot keener than the Americans. 'Julian sold it to me as the dream deal,' explained Sean. 'McCartney himself was going to personally back the team forever, there was an initial seven-year rolling contract, we were going to the Tour. It would be a gravy train for everyone involved.'

Julian made it clear to Sean that he didn't want to get involved in a dutch auction with USPS for his services, but instead made him a firm offer in October.

'I wasn't sure who was working for who at US Postal,' confessed Sean. 'Dirk De Mol, the assistant there, is a real nice bloke. But in the end, Johnny Weltz was squeezed out and Johan Bruyneel came in instead. In the deal offered by Lance, I would have been on level pegging with Johnny, which I wasn't keen on at that time as I was so inexperienced. With Johnny going so soon after, maybe it wasn't such a bad choice to have said no to them.'

The idea of being able to grow with the team at McCartney was a lot more attractive to Sean. He said yes to Julian's offer and became manager of the Linda McCartney cycling team. Sean was lucky to have Keith Lambert join at the same time as his assistant. 'Lego' had been king of the crit circuit in the salad days of the '70s and '80s, and more recently gained himself a reputation as the Alex Ferguson of British cycling management. His Brite team had won *everything* in 1998, leaving people like the Linda McCartney riders to pick up scraps from the top table. Sean readily acknowledged his lack of experience in domestic cycling, having spent his entire career racing abroad, so Keith's touch would be vital.

There was still enough time left in 1998 for some bad feeling within the McCartney ranks. Mark Walsham was intending to retire at the end of the season, and was under the impression that the DS role was his. Julian denied that he had ever offered Walsham the job, and claimed he had merely asked him if he would be interested were the position to become available. Whatever had happened, Walsham went away unhappy at the end of the year.

Julian came into Sigma Sport to see me one day in the autumn and told me about how the team was shaping up for 1999: all the best riders from the soon-to-be-history Team Brite squad, some useful Aussies, Cel, and Sean as the DS. How would I like to be involved? I went away and wrote my own job description: I could get in their sponsors' faces, badger the press, make the team sound big time all the time, look after guests at the proper races and keep them away from the tin-pot trophy events that we'd have to do at times. He made me an offer and I became the part-time press officer of the Linda McCartney Pro Cycling Team.

Chapter 2: With a Little Luck

Linda McCartney died in 1998, finally succumbing to the cancer she had kept at arm's length for years. Her last public appearance had been a photo-shoot with the team, and everybody who had met her had been inspired by her fire and belief. She made it clear to Paul that she was convinced that the cycling team was a perfect vehicle for both her range of foods and her beliefs, and his commitment to the squad following the dark days of her loss was exactly as she had wanted. The team had to deal with the sadness and loss of direction caused by losing their founder and patron, but not with a loss of sponsorship. They would now be racing in Linda's memory.

The goosebumps on Jonny Clay's pasty-white legs were a clear message to all foolhardy souls: do NOT wear shorts in Trafalgar Square in February.

We had our huge Mercedes camper/truck/holiday home fully liveried up and parked on the pavement near one of the four famous lions, just downwind of the National Gallery, mobbed by press and punters alike. It was my first day on the job and I was so far out of my depth that drowning appeared a distinct possibility.

As our impressive new squad lined up for pictures, I attempted to answer the questions fired off by what passes in British cycling circles as a press scrum . . . a few blokes with notebooks. I had three stock answers, which I cleverly rotated to appear more knowledgeable. They were: 'I don't know', 'I'm not sure', and 'I'll check that out for you'. I'd been watching *Father Ted*, you see, and had been particularly impressed by the theory that Ted could get the usually inappropriately behaved Father Jack through an Episcopal inspection by teaching him to answer every question with one of three answers: 'Yes', 'No', or 'That would be an ecumenical matter'. Jack's credibility with the bishops came out of it better than mine with the hacks.

Much of the press attention had been stirred up by rumours of the Fab One himself turning up, but that was to be a forlorn hope. Instead, they got what must have been one of the most impressive domestic cycling team line-ups ever seen in Britain: there was the cream of the previous season's dominators, Team Brite, the best of the rest on the British scene, some tasty Antipodeans and a big scary German.

BEN BROOKS

At only 19, Ben already had a pedigree: he'd been part of the Australian quartet who took gold in the World Junior Team Pursuit a couple of years previously. He always looked amazingly calm and smooth on the bike, displayed a real intelligence in sniffing out races and was definitely a big prospect. There were question-marks over his temperament after a couple of public bust-ups in Australia, but, after all, he was only a teenager.

JULIAN CLARK

There he was, all dressed up in a sparkly gold-and-black kit, the man who had been riding his bike seriously for just a year now one of the big new superteam. That's what you can do when you're the boss! Julian's competitive nature and zest for training meant that he would refuse to be a passenger, though. He'd already finished the Prutour and the Tour of Slovenia, and thought that he could really do something in the 1999 Premier Calendar races.

JONNY CLAY

One of the three old boys who were expected to dominate the season's domestic racing, Jon was 35 by the time of that photo-shoot in Trafalgar Square, but had just completed one of his best-ever seasons. The Archer

Grand Prix, the Girvan Three-Day and the Tour of Lancashire winners' bouquets had all made their way back to Horsforth, and he was an integral part of the successful GB pursuit squad.

RUSSELL DOWNING

'Fonzie' had driven down to the Big Smoke in his white Ford Orion with blacked-out windows . . . the world-renowned Rotherham Ram-raider. Russ was a fast finisher with maximum heart and effort and minimum style: the style could wait till later, he was only 20.

SCOTT GUYTON

Scotty arrived from Rotorua, New Zealand, via the bergs of Flanders. Sean was keen on the idea of a couple of horses in the squad, men that could chase and drive the bunch along for hours at a time in the European races we would be tackling. Quiet, modest and very easy to get along with, he fitted the Yates profile perfectly.

ALLAN IACUONE

Al was seen as our climbing genius, a little Aussie with lungs of steel who could go with the best in the high mountains. Earmarked as one of our 'hitters' for the bigger races, he would live at the Belgian base we had set aside for Scott and the Aussies.

MATT ILLINGWORTH

A prodigious talent with an enormous heart, lungs and capacity for lager evaporation, Matt was the only guy I knew really well, as he was my brother-in-law's best mate and had already proved himself in the testing environment of our local pub many times. He had a string of Commonwealth Games track medals, had been GB ten-mile record holder and always scared the opposition in time trials, but Sean saw him first and foremost as a workhorse like Scott, a battering ram to set up the others in the team.

CHRIS LILLYWHITE

One of British cycling's most prolific winners, Cel was now 32, having been at the top for virtually half his life. Winning the last Milk Race in 1993, and a greedy appetite for the lucrative criteriums of the '80s and early '90s, had earned him the sobriquet of 'The Richest Man in Cycling', which he denied but secretly loved.

DAVE McKENZIE

Macca always seemed to have his head screwed on so tightly, it was hard to believe he was only 24. He was tough, clever and a fearsome sprinter who had given some of our guys a regular view of his backside whilst outdoing them at stage finishes of the Prutour in 1998. He had been on the Australian national squad then, and had also raced in Italy.

CHRIS NEWTON

This Chris was known by all and sundry as 'Junior', even though he was 26 by that time. He was always seen as a hugely talented prospect, and was expected to become our team leader in many of the stage races we would be tackling. He was a great time triallist, a good climber, and had a good enough kick to win lots of one-day races in Britain too.

ROB REYNOLDS-JONES

'The Log' was a kind of pseudo-county type, keen on a cravat and shooting-stick for hunting parties around Bolton Abbey. He was also one of the funniest men I've ever met, with a gentle, self-deprecating irony that everyone loved. Chubby-cheeked that day in Trafalgar Square, he skinnied down quickly and naturally to make the most of his impressive climbing ability. A little fragile for the big races, but nevertheless one of the most popular men in the team.

HEIKO SZONN

You know how they say, 'They broke the mould when they built that one'? Well, Heiko actually appeared to have come out of a mould. The nearest thing to a robot you are ever likely to set eyes upon, Heiko was a law unto himself. He'd got the job by turning up on Sean and Pippa's doorstep and explaining how he was a former German teammate of Jan Ullrich, now living in Kent. Could he have a ride, please? He joined the team on a triallist's contract.

CHRIS WALKER

After Jonny and Cel, our third experienced British hitter. 'Whacker' was 33, but still very much at the top of a tree that had supported the three of them from a previous generation and into this one without blunting their powers. He too had won the Milk Race, hampered though he had been at that time by a horrendous hair-crime, and had shared a podium with Miguel Indurain in Italy that same year. He was now National Criterium Champion. Unlike Cel, he didn't really have any long-term plans left for the continent, having tried his hand abroad with the American Subaru-Montgomery team, but could still dominate at home.

JULIAN WINN

Desperate to cement his reputation as Fastest Welshman, 'Winnie' was probably the hardest worker on the team, always ready to chase a lost cause. His willingness to show his hand sometimes meant that he didn't win as often as he could, but he was always up there, and likely as not it would be his own teammates who would benefit from his efforts. His professional attitude and approach to training were a credit to him.

I was incredibly nervous, not just because I hadn't a clue what I was meant to be doing, but because I was meeting Sean for the first time. I didn't want him thinking I was some kind of tit, and likewise didn't want him to be a disappointment either. The photos finished, we schlepped across past St Martin-in-the-Fields for our celebratory vegetarian lunch in Café Pacifico round the corner. I fell into step beside the big feller.

'Well, I think that went well, don't you? Everybody seems to be getting on well, and there were some good press people there,' I ventured.

'Sorry, do I know you?' he asked. Great start, Deering. You might recognise him from the posters on your bedroom wall when you were a teenager, but he's hardly going to recognise you from your appearance on the subs' bench at the Under-12s Hounslow Cup final, is he?

As it turned out, the lunch was a perfect way for everyone to relax and have fun. I got to know all the guys, plus Adrian Timmis who would be our *soigneur*, and Carl, the new mechanic. The sponsors were well represented too, Tim Treharne there for Linda McCartney and picking up the tab with his platinum Amex card . . . lovely. Thanks to the seating plan, I ended up having an engrossing three-way conversation with the interesting Chris Field and Sigma Sport's Ian Whittingham about bike technology. The new team bikes were being supplied by Chris Field's Hotta company, specialists in carbon fibre technology. They had entered into an agreement with Dunlop, intended to provide the financial muscle for them to march into top-end bike production as big players. They had two main models: one was the one-piece Hotta time-trial frame so beloved of Sean and his Sunday-morning testing buddies, the other was the distinctly gorgeous Perimeter, earmarked to take over the world of professional road racing. However, the Perimeter's suitability was hampered by its sizing – they could only turn it out with one head tube length at that time, meaning that it was only really ideal for time trials. As a result, Dunlop-Hotta had some steel bikes made for the guys to race on . . . they were by far the worst bikes I have ever seen a professional cyclist sit on. At the end of the year, we would do well to get £250 for one.

However, it wasn't long before they were getting results. The team were off to Malaysia for the Tour of Langkawi, the world's fourth richest race after the Tours of France, Italy and Spain. The Malaysian government threw huge pots of cash at the race in an attempt to entice the big teams to venture into the jungle for a race in February, a full month before European racing starts in earnest. It would be one of our biggest races of the whole year, competing against the likes of the giants at Mapei, and an early chance to tap on the shoulders of the European race organisers that we had to impress to get invitations to their races.

Our six-man team was Clark, Iacuone, Illingworth, McKenzie, Newton and Winn, with Sean in charge. The other boys went back to training, I carried on flogging computer bits and waiting eagerly for Sean's daily faxes. We quickly got into a daily routine. Sean's fax would say, 'Nothing much happened, bunch sprint, Macca sixth, everybody OK.' My report would begin, 'Another impressive day for the Linda McCartney Pro Cycling Team as they mixed it with the world's best in some thrilling action . . .' You get the picture. That would get faxed to about 60 different people from the various sponsors and press. Within half an hour it would be up on Stuart Howell's funky new website too: we were getting into a groove with the routine.

At about 6.30 a.m. on the third day of the race, my phone rang. I leapt over Louise, tripped over the dog and slid downstairs on my backside.

'Hello?'

'Hi, John, it's Pippa Yates. Sorry to ring so early, but Sean asked me to: David McKenzie won today.'

In about 30 seconds' time, I think all the neighbours were up too, thanks to my hollering and shouting.

VEGETARIAN VICTORY

We didn't have to wait long for the debut victory – and what a place to take it! Up against some of the world's best, the brand new Linda McCartney Pro Cycling Team swept to an astonishing first and second place in the third stage of the Tour of Langkawi. David McKenzie of Australia pulled off the sprint win the McCartneys had been hoping for, with England's Chris Newton completing a superb 1–2 for the all-vegetarian squad.

'It was the way we did it that was most satisfying,' said a joyful Julian Clark at the finish. 'It's not like we're riding on the coat-tails of the big teams. There was a hill about ten kilometres from the finish and Sean told us to get up the front and put some guys in a bit of trouble. There was Matt Illingworth, Julian Winn, Allan Iacuone, Chris Newton, David McKenzie and myself pulling as hard as we could. We went past Andrea Tafi (Mapei) at about 25 miles an hour up the climb and suddenly the whole field was split by our pressure.'

From then on it was a case of keeping David McKenzie, the team sprinter, in a good position for the finish. 'David climbs better than a lot of the sprinters, so we knew that if we could weed a few of the bigger guys out of the bunch he would be in with a great chance in the sprint,' explained team manager Sean Yates. 'To get second as well was a huge bonus. Chris Newton was our last man leading David out, and he went so hard nobody else could get round him.'

The cycling world has been forced to sit up and take notice of a British-based vegetarian cycling team. What an impact they have made already.

John Deering
Linda McCartney Pro Cycling Team

A team for a week, and already winners! What a great feeling for Macca as he stood on the podium in Kuala Kangsar, his performance already justifying his move to Britain.

It must be said that I had left one itsy-bitsy little thing out of the press release. As the bunch were lining up for the sprint, some of the big names misread some ambivalent signals from race organisation and shot off into the *deviation* for team cars, missing the finish. Junior and Macca had made no such error, launching their move along the right-hand side as the others swung moronically left into the pits.

Julian was absolutely buzzing on the phone. Not only had the team he had newly created won a stage in such a big event, he was actually out there and doing it himself. 'It's unbelievable,' he said, his voice full of the wonderment of an 11 year old at his first cup final. 'The racing is mad – you've got half-a-dozen decent pro teams, some good European national squads, and then 100 guys from South-east Asia who haven't got a clue what's going on. There's one guy from China who gets spat in the first ten miles every day – but he still finishes.

'Today, we went over the top of this climb, and as usual, some local boys wanted to be first over the top. I was right up there, and as we were going down the other side, there were guys switching each other and running off their line in front: before I knew it, the Cantina Tollo rider in front of me had swerved to avoid somebody and put me on the grass. I was bumping down the mountain like a downhill mountain biker. I looked down at my computer and I was doing 58 kph! It only lasted a few seconds, thank God, and I managed to get back on the tarmac.'

So much for the rubbish bikes. I'd never have admitted it to anybody willingly parting with several thousand pounds for a beautiful new racing machine in the shop, but it just goes to show how little difference the bike makes at that level. As long as it goes – so what? The engine is inside the rider.

Within a couple of days, Julian's engine was causing a spot of bother. A virus hit quite a few of the teams, and the boss was forced to pull out with a temperature of 106 degrees. It was a shame for him, but good that we only lost one of the team to it and, anyway, within a day or two he was right as rain again. He was most concerned about not being able to help Allan Iacuone when the race got to the big mountains, as he was one of our better climbers.

Al was going really well. On the 8th of the 12 stages, he made the all-important break that would shape the race, as much of the field lost more than 10 minutes in the hills. He was now in 11th spot, with many of the pre-race favourites way behind him. What's more, the fearsome ascent of the Genting Highlands was still to come, and if he could stay with the big guns, he could push up even further.

Genting is an incredible climb, a soaring 26 kilometres of road up above Kuala Lumpur. It's like a motorway at the bottom, then begins to wind quite a bit, passing the enormous golf hotel and zig-zagging under the cable car line several times before its final few vertiginous hairpins up to the Blackpool-style amusement arcades at the summit.

A break went away early in the shortish stage, with none of the main players involved. When they hit the slopes proper, Sergei Ivanov of TVM launched an all-out attack designed to win the race. The front of the *peloton* splintered; only four riders were able to match the Russian – Rinaldo Nocentini and Paolo Lanfranchi from Mapei, Simensen from Agro Adler . . . and Allan Iacuone from Linda McCartney. Only Ivanov and Lanfranchi were better placed overall than little Al, so he knew that every turn of the pedals was carrying him up the rankings. They stormed past the gates of the golf hotel, hearts close to bursting with the effort, then dog-legged left on to a horrible, dead straight couple of kilometres: dead straight *up* is how it looked. As they swept past some of the remnants of the earlier break, Lanfranchi started to lift the pace even more. It was too much for Al, and he lost contact with the wheel in front, but battled on upwards, concentrating on staying within himself and not blowing up, losing all of those hard-earned seconds.

By the time he struggled over the line on top of the mountain a few minutes later, Allan had climbed his way to third place overall in the world's fourth-richest race. Lanfranchi had done enough to win and Ivanov was second. The following day's criterium in Kuala Lumpur would be little more than a procession: the Linda McCartney team would be heading back to Europe with an enormously successful first race under their belts.

If you were a member of a cycling team struggling for recognition, trying to force its way into people's thinking and justify your sponsors' investment, it would be nice to go to one of those sponsor's houses and see your picture on the wall, wouldn't it? Better still if it was a framed *Cycling* cover of Macca and Junior taking first and second in Malaysia. Even better if that sponsor was by far the most important individual behind your funding. Best of all if he was Sir Paul McCartney.

We drove down to the south coast from the *service course* near Reigate. Well, Sean used to call it the *service course*; most of us thought of it as the-industrial-unit-workshop-type-place. By the time we pitched up in East Sussex, some of us were feeling distinctly groggy from sitting in the back of the swaying camper van for a couple of hours. The Fab One's studio is located in a windmill with fantastic views over the coast . . . incredible place.

'Linda and me were driving along that road down by the sea one day,' he told us, pointing off into the distance. 'We saw this place and immediately thought, "yes, got to have it", then spent the next hour trying to find the road up here. When we finally got to the front door, there was nobody home, so I had a scout round and found a window open round the back. I sat down in the living-room with my chequebook open and waited for somebody to turn up.' You can take the scouser out of Liverpool, but you can't take Liverpool out of the scouser, then.

We had our photos taken with the man himself on his lawn. The photographer had us drive the big Merc camper onto the neatly tended grass as a backdrop. After Paul and the others had gone inside, we removed it, leaving behind the most outrageous trench right across his pride and joy. Sean the gardener was mortified, vainly treading and stamping on the grass as though the earth would somehow remould itself into shape. 'Don't worry, Sean,' someone called out, 'I'm sure he's got another one.'

Sir Paul treated us to two hours in his superb studio. I think we'd all expected a bit of handshaking and some 'well dones', which would have been fine, but instead we got the full works. What a nice fellow. Actually, he seemed genuinely excited to be able to show people round. Most of the guys seemed to be struck dumb for much of the time indoors, so it was largely left to me and Keith Lambert to keep up the team's end of the conversation.

'Still using AC30s then, Paul?' I asked as we walked in, seeing his beautiful vintage '60s Vox amplifier.

'Yeah! D'you play a bit then, mate?' And he was off, advising me to get an old AC30, not a new one, ('We blew up a dozen of the crappy new ones on the last tour'), showing us how the fully automated mixing desk worked, giving us a rundown of his symphonic work-in-progress on his Cubase, even playing us the first demos for the rock 'n' roll album he was doing with Dave Gilmour out of Pink Floyd. Magic.

Best of all was the tour of the instruments. 'I still do most of my writing at the piano,' he explained, sitting down at a beautiful custom-made baby grand whose keys had been done in negative black and white. All of a sudden he was banging out the intro to 'Lady Madonna', and I was pinching myself: 'That's Paul McCartney! Paul McFuckingCartney!!!' We got 'Heartbreak Hotel' on the double bass that was used on the original Elvis 45 – he'd bought it at auction. We got a drum solo on the kit set up by Ringo and an accompanying anecdote about Keith Moon, we got a Ray Charles impression on the electric piano . . . Jesus, you would have thought he was name-dropping if he hadn't been more famous than any of them.

Then he played us some ambient stuff he'd been making with the guys who worked at the studio under the pseudonym of The Fireman, which we all really liked. 'Sounds like you were off your nut when you did this, Paul,' somebody offered. 'Don't do it, kids,' he winked, giving us the famous thumbs up. What a sound bloke – he sent us 15 copies of the CD in the post the very next day with a thank-you letter.

Everybody was nervous by now about getting a place in the team for the Prutour. The Tour of Britain would easily be our biggest race of the year, and a whole lot of pressure would be on us as the No.1 GB team up against the world. There were only six places available and Sean had to decide who would be going.

Chris Walker was flying that spring. A blistering sprint had seen him burst out of the five-man break to win the uphill finish at the Essex Grand Prix, then a great bullying ride with Winnie had seen them take first and third respectively at the Archer near Beaconsfield a few weeks later. In between he managed to take two stages on the Scottish coast at Easter's Girvan Three-Day. He looked a certainty to start the Prutour in Westminster, as did our man for the overall, Chris Newton. Junior had triumphed in the only domestic race we'd tackled that included a time trial: the Europa Two-Day in Hampshire, his second consecutive win there. It was a good testing ground for the shape of the Prutour, which also included a short test against the clock.

Somebody else having fun at the Europa was Jonny Clay. The short time trial was his speciality, and he flew around the tight 6 km time trial circuit faster than anybody else . . . too fast, it would appear, for the marshal who unaccountably walked straight out in front of him as Jon crossed the downhill finish line at a rate of knots. Jonny's right shoulder smashed into the guy as he tried to squeeze between him and the barriers, and the hapless helper was hurled into the air. Somehow, Jonny kept his balance, but the man with the clipboard looked dead. Eventually he came round and was carted off to hospital with a broken wrist and no idea what had hit him. Jonny's painful shoulder stopped him from playing any meaningful part in that afternoon's proceedings, where Junior snatched a time bonus on the finish line to take a narrow victory from *Men's Health*'s impressive Kiwi, Gordon Macauley.

With Whacker's win in the Archer, we had won all four Premier Calendar events, and there were dark mutterings of how Linda McCartney's dominance was bad for the sport. However, it was a different story in France, where we had been to contest the GP Cholet, GP Rennes and Route Adelie, races unheard of in the UK but fiercely fought over by the French Tour de France hopefuls. Some of us thought that Cel and Macca could really well do over there, but we were to be proved optimistic – frankly, we got hammered. The gap between UK and French racing was more like a gulf.

Matt Illingworth was writing a diary for our website, and he let people know what it was really like over there. At the GP Cholet, our first Coupe de France race, he got well and truly hammered up and down the little Flandrian-type hills that the French call *bosses*:

> The race was 202 km long around twisting lanes, with the 'Challenge 10 *Bosses*', and I tell you, these ten *bosses* were definitely running the show. When you're weighing in at a slender 130 kg and someone says you've got to ride along dirt tracks and go up and down the ten *bosses*, you're not going to be best pleased. The race was a lot harder than I thought it was going to be, because I wasn't planning on having a pair of legs on that felt like they'd been beaten with rubber pipes after the first climb and getting spat out forever at 110 km, *Bosse 6*. Jonny and the rest of the team were with me by 170 km. The only exception was Chris Newton, who managed to finish, but he was so cold at the end he looked like he'd spent the five hours in a fridge.
>
> At least we were all consistent: we all got belted at the same

time and Sean did say he wanted us represented in every group.
Mind you, I think he meant the front group, not the back one.
About 40 riders got round in the end and it was a very tough race
to start the season with. Jan Kirsipuu won for the third year in a
row and I remember Sean saying he couldn't climb a hump-back
bridge. Well, he might struggle on a hump-back bridge, but his
two-kilometre-ten-per-cent-berg riding isn't too bad.

David McKenzie was a cert for the Prutour too, but somebody else who
should have been considered a definite starter was struggling for form.
Since coming back from Malaysia, Allan Iacuone was going like the
proverbial sack of potatoes. Eventually, Sean had to bite the bullet and
decide that Al's form was not going to come round in time for May, and
he left him out of the starting line-up.

Heiko was a complete enigma. Seemingly impervious to advice or
directions from his manager, be it Keith Lambert in the UK races or Sean
on the French trips, he was still clearly enormously strong. At the Circuit
de Sarthe he lost less than a minute in the big time trial to the man about
to win his first Tour de France, Lance Armstrong. However, at the
Lincoln Grand Prix, he went out of his way to rile Keith. Having made
the 11-man selection along with Chris Newton, who had a good record
of success in the race, he blatantly disobeyed Lego's instructions by
working when he wasn't meant to, and sitting on when Keith wanted
him to ride.

'Just look at the big lump,' moaned Keith to me in the back seat of the
'A' Class. 'He's always riding in a gear twice as big as anyone else, he's never
sitting on the saddle, he's either first-in-line or last-in-line, he hates a corner
. . . I don't know what to do with him.' The word on the street was that
Heiko had suffered a really serious accident a few years ago, and hated
riding in the bunch now. That would certainly explain his strange
positioning: at the front, at the back or alongside, but never in the middle.

Keith drove up to the bunch and told Chris and Heiko to sit on and
not do any work, as there were teams better placed than us in the break
and we had a reinforcement in Rob Reynolds-Jones coming up from

behind. After dropping back to check on Log's progress, Lego took us back up to the break. To his amazement, they were stretched out in a long line, all hanging on to the wheel in front. And the man doing the damage at the front? You've got it: Heiko.

'I don't believe this!' he whispered in apoplexy. Gaining permission from the race *commissaire* to move forward, Keith manoeuvred the 'A' Class alongside the break. Leaning out of his driver's window, he let Heiko have the full benefit of his wisdom. 'I've fucking had enough of you, Heiko!' he shouted in his thick Bradford brogue, veins popping on his neck. Ten other faces wearing helmets all looked to their left in total amazement at Lego's outburst, but Heiko just notched it up a gear, bowled along out of the saddle and shrugged his shoulders as if to say, 'Whatever.' A few minutes later, he would be slipping his chain at the foot of the final ascent of the cobbled Michaelgate up to the line, missing out on a chance to affect the outcome. Rather than going for the win himself, Lego would have preferred to see Heiko doing more to help Chris Newton take the victory. As it was, Junior was only able to manage sixth behind French-based Lithuanian, Salius Ruskis. In third spot was a name we would come to see more of: Ireland's Ciaran Power. That was Heiko's last race for Linda McCartney.

There was another reason for Lego to be stressed that day. It was the final weekend of the Nationwide League season, and his beloved Bradford City were in with a shout of making the Premiership for the first time in their less than illustrious history. However, to do it, they needed to get a result at Wolves. Thus, for much of the race, we had two radios blaring: race radio keeping us in touch with events around us, and Five Live giving us the latest from Molineux. When the final whistle blew, they had scraped home, and Keith went berserk. Only thing was, we were about 5 km from the finish by then, and he only just managed to keep the Mercedes under control with all his leaping around and celebrating in the driver's seat.

Matt Illingworth became GB ten-mile champion in Dorset, giving Sean a timely nudge about his own good form. His only regret was that I said he came from Southend in the press release. 'It's Westcliff! Westcliff!' he complained. Snob.

The other likely Prutour starters were in Slovenia. Chris Walker and Chris Lillywhite were going very well out there, with Cel in particular taking a string of top placings in what was an extremely hard race. Sean's Prutour team was virtually fixed in his mind now, with Slovenia his last race to decide. We were taking on the Irish Milk Ras concurrently with the Prutour, so there would be good racing to come for everybody.

One day in Slovenia necessitated a horrible long transfer in the team cars in a severe rainstorm. The whole race drove in convoy, our two maroon Mercedes estate cars somewhere in the middle. To ease the ennui in Sean's car, Winnie was reading out loud from a recent *FHM* containing a story about women's darkest fantasies. 'He was doing the voices and everything, me and Scotty were getting well uncomfortable in the back seat,' said Julian. 'I pushed the toilet door shut,' continued Winnie in his best Tara Palmer-Tomkinson impression, 'and raised one foot up to stand on the bowl. Looking deep into his eyes, I began to slowly pull my skirt up my thighs, and then –'

BANG!

Sean had driven straight up the back of the car in front. Cel was out of team car two and around the scene in a flash. Before the red-faced occupants of team car one could even get their seatbelts undone, he was standing hands-on-hips, assessing the damage and tutting. 'Lot of work, that. Hell of a lot of work.'

Chapter 3: The Long and Winding Road

Sean settled upon his six for Westminster. They would be all the Christophers: Newton, Lillywhite and Walker; Matt Illingworth; Dave McKenzie; and Julian Winn. In the end, it was only Winnie's place that was really in doubt, with Sean deciding that he was showing better form than Jonny or Allan, and that his record of a stage win in the previous year's edition made him a better bet than taking another workhorse like Scott to complement Matt.

The Prutour would be my first full-time week with the team. I was to drive the 'A' Class throughout the race, taking guests drawn from our sponsors and the press on the race with me each day. I was in heaven, as you can imagine. Not least because it meant I got my own Zenith watch at last. All the guys had been presented with Zeniths as part of their sub-sponsor's deal with the team at the start of the year, and now I was to get my hands (or at least my wrist) on one of the two-grand beauties. I didn't realise that I'd have to give it back in a week's time, though. Doh!

The organisation for the Prutour was absolutely fantastic, 'the best in the world after the Tour de France', according to Sean. I raised an eyebrow at him placing the Tour of Britain in front of those of Italy and Spain, but he explained that in those countries, the public is much more aware and understanding of bike racing – they don't need to put such an effort into getting things right. In the UK, road closures for a bike race are a total head-scratcher for most people, so you've got to be right on the ball. That was proved in 1998 when a motorcycle policeman was tragically killed, hit by a motorist who had found his way on to the route.

The night before the first-stage circuit race around Westminster, we were billeted in the sumptuous surroundings of the Heathrow Ramada. In fact, the race had taken over virtually all the hotels on that strip of the A4 along the airport's northern perimeter. The locals gawped in amazement at the sheer number of vehicles and personnel involved when professional bike racing comes to town. This being my old 'manor', I was only too delighted to show off my funky Linda McCartney 'A' Class, but on the way out of the Ramada car park, I made faux pas No.1. Those cars have a lovely semi-automatic gearbox with no clutch. As I rummaged for the change needed to escape the car park, I forgot about that, and instead of putting the car into second gear from first, I stamped on the brake and not the non-existent clutch. I can still see the imprint of my forehead in the roof. Ouch.

Back in Sean's hotel room, we all bunched in to watch Pantani take on the first real mountain stage of the Giro. Up they went, across the snow line, Baldie piling on the pressure until only Gotti could hold his wheel. Pantani gave him such a dirty look for hanging on that Gotti tried to do the decent thing by coming through and giving *il Pirata* a turn. Within seconds, Pantani had got his breath back, overtaken the former winner, and danced off over the horizon. What a display.

The boys who had been racing for us at Settimana Bergamasca a few weeks earlier were amazed at how well some of their opponents from then were now going. 'Look at that!' said Macca, pointing in incredulity at one of the better-known Italians scaling the mountain, 'he was creeping at Bergamasca! *Creeping!*' A few knowing looks did the rounds. That's the sort of thing you're up against when British teams go and race in Europe, sudden 'unaccountable' surges in form for the big races.

Westminster was fantastic, one of the best days out imaginable. Thousands of people thronged Whitehall to see the start of the race, giving the lie to the idea that cycling is unpopular in Britain. It may not have the same universal appeal as, say, football, but the people who do like it love it passionately.

Cel was absolutely flying that day. Knowing full well there was live TV coverage on Channel 4 all afternoon, he got in a break and rode off the front for nearly all the race, picking up some handy sprint bonuses en route. When the break looked about to be captured he took off on his own, picking up more valuable airtime for Linda McCartney, Motorola, Zenith Watches and Dunlop-Hotta. At one stage, after taking another intermediate sprint, it even looked as though he could wear the leader's jersey that night, but eventually he was swallowed up by a chase from the big Rabobank and Credit Agricole squads. Now it was time to regroup and see if we could fire David McKenzie to a stage win. The whole team massed on the front, stretching the whole *peloton* into a long snaking line with their speed. Matt did a massive turn, Whacker chucked one in, Junior and Winnie were there and even Cel managed another effort. It was a fantastic sight for Sean and me as we looked on from the pit lane on the corner of Parliament Square and Whitehall. On the last lap, Credit Agricole moved up to take on the train, but they didn't have quite enough speed when they turned on to The Embankment into the headwind, and everybody got a little bit swamped as the front of the race slowed fractionally. Round the last corner past Big Ben and back into Whitehall, it was Leon Van Bon of Rabobank who was best placed, and he was first to the line by the Cenotaph, closely pursued by George Hincapie and Stuey O'Grady. Macca was fourth – we thought that was pretty good in that sort of company. What's more, we had ridden like the proper continental outfit we aspired to be, and let the big teams know who we were.

The atmosphere before, during and after the stage was electric, with the team mobbed by every type of fan. There were people there just for the spectacle and a day out, there were those who enjoyed the opportunity to see some of the riders they only get to see on telly at the Tour in the flesh, and there were the fully fledged 'nyrons' who were totally obsessed with cycling, yet somehow seemed to derive so little pleasure from it. Matt Illingworth described a nyron for somebody not *au fait* with the McCartney slang: 'They like to hang around bike races, especially time trials, that's their natural habitat. Often they'll be old boys dressed in pre-1960s track tops, which are far too small for them, finished off with a rather dashing pair of grey slacks raised at least two inches above their non-branded trainers, showing off the good old white socks. They stand in front of the result board and write down all the times on the start sheet: that sits on a clipboard with a stopwatch on it, a spare pencil in case number one pencil breaks, a pencil sharpener in case number one and number two pencils break and of course a rubber. If you're a '90s bike spotter, you'll have digital timing, two pens and a bottle of Tipex.'

One chap came up to Chris L. with a very serious look on his face and asked, 'What sort of average speed did you manage today?'

'Sorry,' replied Cel, 'I don't use a computer on my bike, so I'm not sure.'

'Do you think you'll be able to keep that average speed up for the rest of the race?' the fellow asked earnestly. There was a pause.

'Sorry, I don't use a computer on my bike, so I'm not sure.'

Another curio from that day was a row over a jersey. It wouldn't be the last, but it bore more than a passing resemblance to a discussion we would be having with the cycling authorities almost a year later to the day. Chris Walker, as National Criterium Champion, was taking advantage of a rare opportunity to wear the special champion's jersey that Impsport, our clothing manufacturers, had made for him. That meant there were two white jerseys with a blue and red hoop in the race, as Matt Stephens of the Harrods team was wearing his National Road Race Champion's jersey too. That was one jersey too many for the man from the UCI, who said that the stage wasn't a crit after all, it was just a normal road race that happened to go round a small circuit 40 times. This sounded an awful lot like a crit to us.

In years gone by, Whacker would have been showing off that jersey at least one evening a week as he toured the country's lucrative crit circuit. However, the dearth of events like that by 1999 meant that this was one of the few chances he'd have to tell people that he was the champ at this sort of thing. So what the hell, we went ahead, judging that the extra publicity would be worth it: we'd forked out to get the thing specially made, after all. We got fined.

The race snaked across the south-east, down from Rochester to

Portsmouth, then onwards and westwards the following day, from Winchester up to Bristol. Heading into Pompey in the most outrageous headwind along the seafront at Southsea, there was a huge pile-up. Some bright spark had designed the run-in to involve a 90-degree bend immediately after the one-kilometre-to-go banner, simultaneously halving the width of the road. The headwind meant that the front of the bunch was quite wide as they swept towards the finish, all trying to find room for the sprint. As the road unexpectedly narrowed, a number of riders found themselves with nowhere to go but the barriers. Cel, wearing the purple jersey of sprints leader, smacked straight into the metal, snapping his two-day-old bike in half and twatting his knee in the process.

'It was a horrible colour anyway,' he grinned. He was right, too: all the six had been given new bikes for the Prutour, a grade or nine better quality steel than the Black Shadows some unscrupulous frame builder had striped Dunlop-Hotta up with at the start of the year. Most were a groovy yellow-orange blend to match the jersey, but the pantone codes must have got muddled for Cel's and Winnie's . . . 'copper mix' is probably how Freemans catalogue would have described them. 'Runny turd' was the team's verdict. So for all his efforts, Cel would be back on the Black Shadow for Stage Three.

Stage Three would be the platform for a fantastic ride from David McKenzie. It was 171 km, with three nasty climbs in the back half of the race, not ideal sprinters' territory, but Macca wasn't to be deterred. I think somebody has already mentioned how Dave can climb better than the other sprinters, so he saw the finish on Clifton Down as a good opportunity. By the time the race reached the picturesque slopes of Cheddar Gorge, Macca was in a 12-man break with all the big teams represented. The group split over the long haul up, but Macca chased well over the top and got back on to what was now a seven-man group. Attack and counter-attack followed, with two of Macca's future teammates, Bjornar Vestol and Mirko Puglioli, punching their weight. US Postal's Benoit Joachim went clear over the top of Limeburn Hill. Macca's group were 20 seconds adrift, but the main bunch were way back, well over three minutes in arrears. There was bound to be a big shake-up in the standings overnight now, with leader Leon Van Bon stranded back down the road, and defending champion Stuart O'Grady labouring at an astonishing eight minutes. Macca and Van Bon's Rabobank teammate Marc Wauters drove the chase of the Luxembourger Joachim, Wauters' eyes on the leader's red jersey, which would pass to him from Van Bon if they managed to recapture Joachim. Joachim struggled on. He had all the style of a man pedalling on flat tyres and square wheels, jaw hanging slackly open with the effort of pulling his uncoordinated body forward, but it was working. Macca countered on the slopes of the steep climb up from the banks of the Avon to the finish on Clifton Down, clawing back at Joachim, but looking as though it would be too late to catch him. The US Postal boy hung on gamely for the win, while Macca outsprinted Wauters and Puglioli to take a superb second place on the stage. With a fifth and a tenth already against his name, that was enough to give our man the coveted green jersey of points leader, the most consistent finisher in the race. He was also now third overall, just behind Wauters and a little bit further back from the brave Joachim.

Unsurprisingly, Dave wasn't able to hang on to the third spot over the following day's mountains that led us to Swansea. The stage that had been viewed from the start as the defining shake-up saw the race split to smithereens, with future Tour de France star Raimondas Rumsas conquering the big hills better than anyone else. Junior climbed up into 11th place as the top ten started to take a more settled look.

I spent the day with a very interesting guy called Peter. His wife had won a competition to spend the day in the team car with Sean, who had to mind his language and drive courteously for a few hours. I transported her husband and a journo or two over the route. Peter was in his 60s but full of life – mainly because it was a new-found one. In 1987, he'd been out enjoying a spin round the lanes when his front wheel became jammed between two concrete slabs on a level crossing. Instead of the usual 'plugging' that you might expect in such an accident, the whole bike pivoted on that front wheel and sent Peter crashing down on the side of his head. His neck was broken. The next few years saw Peter completely wheelchair bound and paralysed from the neck down. However, here we were, 12 years on, and he was striding up the impossibly steep Constitution Hill leaving me puffing in his wake, and thinking to myself, 'I *must* get fitter: here's a man who can teach me a bit about making the most of your health.'

Constitution Hill in Swansea is seriously steep, 1-in-3 they reckon: steep enough for Roger Legeay to stall the Credit Agricole team car in front of a huge crowd of laughing *Twin Town* extras, anyway. The locals gave him a push to get started again . . . I forgot to check if the hubcaps were still on afterwards.

That night was eventful. Firstly, we crammed into Matt and Cel's room to watch the European Cup final. Everyone was getting behind Man U, everyone that is except Cel and me. 'I don't want them to win any other week, why should I want them to win now?' is how Cel put it. Tel, our second *soigneur* for the race, was one of those who simply could not believe what he was hearing. 'They're Germans,' he said with astonishment, 'how could you possibly support the *Germans*?' He spat the word out as if it tasted bad.

What's more, Cel had a history with Germans. At the Bank race in Australia one year, a popular end-of-season jaunt for Chris, he'd had a little bit of argy-bargy with a German rider. Seems that said German had one of his countrymen and teammates in a break up the road, and Cel's team were desperately trying to chase the move down. The first German, let's call him Hans, begins trying his best to break the chase up, getting in amongst them and slowing them down. This is seen in cycling circles as pretty underhand, and tends to rile people you might not want to rile in other circumstances. Eventually, former Chelsea hooligan Lillywhite loses his cool and, riding alongside Hans, takes one hand off the bars and delivers an almighty swipe right across his chops. Hans's nose explodes like a Roman candle, blood everywhere. Unfortunately for our have-a-go hero, the momentum of his attack sends him sprawling across the tarmac at high speed, disco'ing the old shoulder and relieving him of a great deal of skin. 'It hurt so bad I could hardly see, but I managed to get to the finish,' remembers the violent-when-pushed Londoner. 'Of course, when I get to the end, he's come looking for some more, but I'm not interested then, am I? All the adrenaline's gone, me arm's hanging down by me side. I turn into a scouser, all "calm down, calm down, mate", until he storms off in a huff.'

Of course, the famous game at wherever-it-was ends in disappointment for Bayern Munich's two new fans, and Tel and I went out for a beer or two in Mumbles. On our return, we were a little bit surprised to find Chris Walker in the hotel car park. The poor old feller looked like he'd seen a ghost, so we sat him down and tried to get him to speak. It turned out that Chris had suffered something that happens to him very occasionally at that time of year, a serious asthma attack, and had gone outside to try and catch his breath.

Tel took him back upstairs and put him back to bed, but it looked bad for the next stage, and that's how it proved. Chris abandoned early on with breathing difficulties and spent the rest of the day in the team car before heading back to Sheffield. In fact, it was a crappy day all round, as we lost Macca's green jersey under dubious circumstances. The longest and hottest day of the race saw us wind all the way up from Swansea across South Wales and the Midlands as far as Birmingham. A break of guys not affecting the overall positions went away early on, shaping the whole course of the day. O'Grady was in there, and managed to salvage a stage win for his disappointment at not being able to defend his overall title from 1998. However, for the Linda McCartney team, the objective was protecting Dave's green jersey from the close attentions of Juris Silovs of the Danish Home-Jack & Jones squad. As the main contenders swung into Cannon Park for the finish, the Mroz boys were on the front for Rumsas, Matt and the others were lining up Macca and Silovs was tucked in behind. Just then, an experienced marshal who really should have known better began signalling to the cars following behind the riders that they should swing right, into the *deviation*. Of course, when a man in a bright yellow bib standing in front of you starts directing you to turn right, you tend to do just that, and Matt led the boys unwittingly into the car park. Silovs cruised through to take fifth place on the stage and nick the jersey off a crestfallen Macca.

It wasn't our last car disaster of the day. We spent the next four hours sat in a traffic jam on the M6, riders cramping with 214 km still in their legs from the day's exertions. There was still room for a little weary banter though, as we blamed the delays on caravans heading north, and by implication, Lego and his own love for the tow-around outdoor life. 'Lovely spot for caravan, Margaret' was his favourite saying. He'd even stopped in the middle of races to point out a nice flat bit of grass next to a picturesque lake or some such beauty spot. The other thing was he said it 'cara*van*', rather than '*car*avan', as the rest of us normal types would.

Poor old Winnie. He launched a do-or-die all-out effort on the run-in to the next day's finish in Blackpool. As he swung on to the seafront with a mile to go, he found himself pounded by a force-eight headwind, and was swallowed up by the bunch, his victory bid over.

Lucky old Winnie. He wasn't concentrating when he'd launched the attack: Hincapie and Wadecki were a further minute up the road. Had he managed to hold off the chasing bunch, Winnie would have been giving his full-on victory salute . . . for third place. Durrrrr.

We finished our Prutour in a wet and windy Edinburgh the following night in some style, the team once again proving more than adept at controlling the speed in a tight-circuit race. Our boys led the bunch in a yellow line for many, many laps, Dave eventually taking another fourth behind the illustrious trio of Julian Dean, Nikolai Bo Larsen and future world No.1 Erik Dekker. Chris Newton finished 12th, a position he would have hoped to have bettered, but pretty satisfactory when you looked at the names ahead of him. He was the best-placed British rider. Rabobank's Marc Wauters was the winner, the Dutch team stealing the jersey off US Postal by attacking en masse for an early-morning intermediate sprint carrying a small time bonus. Wauters would go on to wear the yellow jersey in the Tour de France within a couple of years.

All the team were flying to America out of Edinburgh the following morning, while Sean, mechanic Jon Fry and I drove back to Reigate that night in the little Mercedes 'A' Class. It was a long, long drive, giving me the chance to have a good chat with Sean. People call him shy and unwilling to talk or even make out that he's a bit dim, but that's certainly not my impression. Once you get him going, he'll happily talk for hours on virtually any subject. I quizzed him about his best day in the Tour (the time trial win in Wasquehal, '88), worst day in the Tour (Chiapucci's epic ride to Sestriere in '91), hardest climb (the summit finishes at Plat d'Adet or Superbagneres in the Pyrenees) and his best-ever ride (fifth place at Paris-Roubaix in 1994).

It was a good chance to find out his view on the team's performance, too. I was surprised to discover that he was disappointed with Chris Newton, as I thought he had ridden well. 'He's overweight,' was his surprising analysis. I would later discover that any rider not sporting ribs like a xylophone was considered overweight by the boss. He was very pleased with David McKenzie, who he always felt rode to his maximum despite not being as talented as some. He thought that Dave would never be able to beat the fastest sprinters, but was clever enough to find other ways to win. Illingworth had done well, especially in the stages where he was expected to be strong, like the crits, but lacked a bit of confidence in himself at times. Cel's crash had taken the edge off his great form, but he was always a great leader, motivator and captain in the bunch. Winnie was strong, but sometimes showed his hand too easily. He could do with a bit more craft but was an asset to the team.

I ended up with Sean's Land Rover for a few days as the boys jetted off to Philadelphia for the US Pro Championships, a race that Sean had won. That was handy for me, as Dipper (my band) had a gig in Fulham that weekend, and there was no way I could get all the gear in my old Beetle.

Matt Illingworth sent home his report of racing stateside:

> Woke up the morning after the Prutour ended with a bit of a sore head on board, not being able to remember if it was the hard riding during the previous week or because I'd had a few beers. Maybe I'd just ridden so hard, I'd got amnesia.
>
> Anyway, it was off to the airport, smelling like a brewery and out to America for a shopping trip and three bike races, if we had time to fit them in. Most of the places we've been racing in this

year we've had trouble with the language, so I went to evening classes to brush up on my American. Stuff along the lines of: 'God damn it, what's your friggin' problem, maaaan?'

Within 24 hours, one of the not-so-bright members of our team, Scott Guyton, who is actually one half of a duo we call Dim and Dimmer, the other member being Julian Winn, decided he wanted to peroxide his hair. So, he rushes off to a pharmacy in the 'hood and comes back with this hair dye and the pair of them start to mix it up. Of course, actually reading the label was far too sensible and seeing as neither of them had used hair dye before they knew exactly how to do it. For about three quarters of an hour, Scott is sitting there with a shower cap on his head and smoke coming off his burning scalp, only to eventually remove it and have a perfect head of ginger hair. How uncool is that? Being of low intelligence, he decided if he dyed it four more times with the same stuff it would definitely go white. By now he looked like a Duracell battery, a flat one mind, because his brain wasn't working and as he's got big hair, he looked like a ginger Andrew Ridgeley. What with walking around in red silky tennis shorts, white vest and black leather fingerless gloves, his credibility as being a member of a pro cycling team was looking bad. He also started to miss training because he had to practice his dance routines and was last seen diving into the roof-top swimming-pool singing 'Club Tropicana'.

The first two races were run off at breakneck speed, one being hilly and one being flat. I rode the first one, the First Union Invitational, which sounds like a golf tournament, but is actually a bike race. It was 93 miles, on a hilly circuit where the bunch was going too fast. I got left behind after a few laps, retiring to the hotel room for cookies and Dr Peppers. Next day was a spare day to recover from the flight, so we went out with 'Man of Steel' Sean and got our fortnightly beating off him just to let us know who's in charge.

Race two, the First Union Classic, was on a flat course going up and down the same road, with a loop at either end of the circuit, and was 93 miles as well, run off at just over three hours. Just to make the race more exciting they'd put the circuit in the shady part of town. As we drove in, there were loads of boarded-up shops and people on the street drinking booze out of paper bags. A bit like me in the winter, really. Their idea of fun was to drop rocks on our heads as we went under the bridge every lap, or if they didn't like heights, just lob them from the roadside. So there's 150 riders dodging rocks, while riders who've been dropped are coming back the other way dressed in full downhill mountain biker body armour for protection.

Everyone went pretty good here, so it was roll on Sunday for the big one. The USPRO Championships, a 250km race which goes up the legendary Manayuk Wall ten times, with 750,000 Yanks screaming and shouting, blowing whistles, ringing bells and causing general mayhem whilst getting absolutely bladdered at the side of the road.

This race is pretty massive with Joe Public here, it had live TV all day, unlike the UK where everyone just moans about 'bloody cyclists' and we might get half an hour on the box at 3 a.m. The race started and after at least ten seconds some long-haired American, riding on one of those bikes with a built-in trampoline-style bouncing beam, goes sprinting off down the road like a wild bull. This carried on for the whole event and it was a pretty rapid affair with Macca riding like the star he is and running top 15. Really cool bike race to ride and there's nothing more refreshing than lying on the grass after the event, semi-conscious, drinking a bottle of ice-cold beer and trying to find your way back to the hotel, half-cut.

Julian had absolutely loved what he saw in the USA. 'We were treated like rock stars over there, it was incredible,' he told me on the phone when they got back. 'I've got something I want to talk to you about, let's meet up.'

Julian had a new plan. He had already hinted at wanting 2000 to be a big step up on 1999, and he was having some ideas on how to do it. 'I always thought that a new team's aim should be getting into the Tour de France, but now I'm not so certain,' he began. 'If there's more drug trouble at the Tour this year, the sport is going to be dead on its feet.' The 1998 Tour de France had been a shocking coming of age for riders, administrators and fans alike. The Festina team had been thrown out of the race for drug taking, police raids, abandonments and riders' strikes had continued unabated in a hail of unfriendly press that seemed destined to bring the race, and by extension the sport, to its knees.

'My plan is to split the team in two for next year. Let's run a similar programme to this year, UK racing and French Cup events, but with a smaller squad. Then we'll send another team to the US to race their crit circuit and their stage races. Linda McCartney Foods are launching in America in the New Year, so it will be the perfect vehicle for them.'

This was all making a great deal of sense to me. The team had gained much more interest in the general media in the USA than we had managed in Britain, although it wasn't for want of trying. It appeared that they were more willing to come to *us* over there, while in Britain I hammered doors all day.

'I'm going to pack up racing at the end of this year. It looks like I need a hernia op, anyway,' said Julian. 'I'll run the team full time in Europe, but I want you to go to America and run the business side of things there.'

Things were looking up.

Chapter 4: Live and Let Die

In 1993, when Lance Armstrong was 21, he became World Road Race Champion in a hideous rainstorm in Oslo. Already recognised as a major talent, the young, brash Motorola star had now truly arrived. His impetus to his American team was such that they persuaded Sean Yates to set aside his thoughts of retirement for a couple of years – Sean was the perfect foil for the impetuous Texan, a wise head to point Lance in the right direction, but a good enough rider to be at his side at the crucial stage of the big races.

In 1996, Lance won the first of the hilly Ardennes classics, Fleche Wallonne, then only lost its bigger brother, Liege–Bastogne–Liege, to the crafty skills of the experienced Pascal Richard. When Richard was picking up the gold medal at the Atlanta Olympic Road Race, Armstrong was a disappointing 12th, not what was intended for the pre-race favourite racing on home soil, especially when he was racing in the memory of the late Fabio Casartelli, the last Olympic champion. Motorola rider Casartelli had lost his life the previous summer as he descended the Col de Portet d'Aspet in the Tour de France, Armstrong emotionally taking a stage a couple of days later for his tragically missing teammate.

Unbeknown to him, Lance was racing at Atlanta under the shadow of a malignant testicular cancer that would take him to within an inch of his life. His struggle back from the brink of death to success in the Tour de France is a story that transcends cycling and touches everybody. Lance's story is well told in his book, *It's Not About The Bike*, but his story was also to play a large, though unknowing, part in the Linda McCartney team's story.

After a horrendous battle with cancer and chemo, Lance returned to racing in 1998 but immediately ran into troubles. He was worried that he could never be the man he had been and struggled with his motivation. However, a long training camp and focusing break with his mentor and coach, Chris Carmichael, left the Texan hungry for the sport once again. A miraculous return to racing with successive brilliant fourth places at the Tour of Spain, the World Championship Time Trial and the World Championship Road Race at the back end of 1998 showed Lance that he wasn't just back – he was *better* than he had been before he got sick. He could win the Tour de France. Once deemed too big in build to ever seriously challenge in the high mountains, the new post-cancer slimline Armstrong battered his rivals into submission in the 1999 Tour, setting the scene for his domination of the foreseeable future. But Lance did more than save his own life and career. He resurrected an entire sport. Cycling was down on its knees after the humiliating scenes of 1998 – never has any race needed a hero more than the 1999 Tour de France. They didn't just get a hero, they got a saviour, back from the edge of the grave in swaggering, audacious attacking style, one of the most charismatic figures the game had ever seen. Soon, even the notoriously ambivalent American public had taken their boy to their hearts with his tear-jerking story, and a star was truly born. Only Tiger Woods is a more recognised sporting figure in the USA than Lance Armstrong.

What did that mean to us? Firstly, it meant that the Tour de France dream was very much back on. Plan B, our stateside sojourn, returned to the back burner.

'I've decided to move the whole thing to Europe: it's the only way we can succeed,' explained Julian in August. There were lots of good reasons for this. The first one was undoubtedly the expense. The cost of running a European programme out of Reigate was outrageously prohibitive in property costs and travel. All the vehicles – usually two team cars and a truck – would have to drive to races by ferry. Riders would fly from wherever they were in the UK. In some cases, this led to jaw-dropping airfares to get people like Chris Newton from

Newcastle to Denmark or Rome. Secondly, we wanted to be taken seriously as an international force, and that meant signing riders who could get us into big races and then make an impression. It was hard to imagine anyone leaving a top European team to come and live in England, or race organisers taking our applications seriously while they still had an English address in them.

'I want you to come and work with me full time,' said Julian to me. 'I want you to keep hammering the press, hammering the sponsors, but I'm going to need help day to day in the office too. What do you think?'

I was delighted. But what about Louise? 'She's a masseur, isn't she? Let's check her out.' Louise was indeed an excellent masseur and *soigneur*, although she'd been making a fairly successful career for herself in sales for the last few years. I had met a lot of the people I knew in cycling through her. She had her BCF coaching qualifications and a great schoolgirl cycling record behind her, but she had largely lost interest in the sport through her 20s, just keeping her hand in by looking after a few cyclists and triathletes near us in Kingston. Julian asked her for a massage without letting on that he had higher plans for her, and she came through with flying colours. He followed that up with an invitation to work for the team on the late season trips to Brittany and Denmark, where she quickly slipped into her role as popular *soigneur*.

I don't think I would be revealing too many secrets by saying that Louise and I had not been getting along too well. By 1999 we had been married for four years and the last two were tough to say the least. It was nothing you could put your finger on, or any specific wrongdoing by either one of us, but a general malaise and mistrust that saw us leading increasingly separate existences, forever arguing and making up. The gaps between the arguments and the make-ups grew ever longer. When the team offered both of us a contract to go and work abroad, we were both delighted: maybe this was an opportunity for us to put all our troubles behind us and start afresh?

There was a personal decision for me to make. My band, Dipper, had been offered a smallish recording contract by an independent record company, and as part of the deal would be flown to America for a month's recording. Taking the McCartney job would knock that on the head. How frustrating: you wait all your life for chances like these to come along, and then two turn up at once. I weighed up the options and decided that the McCartney offer held far more promise in the long term, and reluctantly relegated Dipper to the back burner for the immediate future. Darrell and Graham, my bandmates, had never been over-confident about the record deal anyway, worrying that things might not turn out to be as rosy as they appeared, and agreed I should have a go in France.

Julian would run the commercial side of the business, with me as his assistant and looking after PR. Sean would be the *directeur sportif* in Europe, while Keith would run an Under-23 UK squad, designed to prove our commitment to grassroots cycling in Britain with the main squad absent. Chris Lillywhite was retiring from racing, but would assist both Sean and Keith. *Soigneurs* and mechanics were hard to come by – Julian was unhappy with Adrian's performance in '99, considering him to be 'lazy', while we had lost two mechanics: Carl had just found the travelling too much and preferred to spend some time with his family, and his replacement, Jon Fry, had simply disappeared when the going got tough. Fortunately, we had made a great find. Craig Geater was an old Kiwi mate of Scott's who had been staying with him in Belgium for a bit of racing. He owned a bike shop with his mum back in Rotorua, and was a red-hot mechanic and wheelbuilder, so he, like Louise, had stepped in at short notice for that Brittany and Denmark trip and done a fantastic job. He was offered a full-time mechanic's job for 2000. Completing the backroom team was Eddie Wegelius. His brother, Charley, had long been a great prospect in the GB Junior ranks, and was now carving a career for himself as a pro at the world-famous Mapei Institute for young riders. Eddie had already *soigneured* at the highest French amateur level with Vendee U, who would metamorphose into the successful Bonjour pro outfit. He and Louise looked an excellent young partnership in the *soigneur's* car.

The next task was to find a base for this new set-up. Belgium was mentioned, as were northern Spain and the South of France. Much of the programme looked likely to revolve around Italy, where Sean was making good headway with contacts and race organisers, so Spain looked to be a little isolated. Belgium looked OK, but who wants to live there when you can have the South of France? Then there was more narrowing-down to be done. We wanted an international airport, so Nice was a distinct possibility: Sean had lived there for years working with 7-Eleven and Motorola; Lance and his ex-pat American gang were there as a result. Toulouse had an international airport too, plus there was a big English-speaking buzz going on down there – Stuey O'Grady, David Millar, Jay Sweet and Jeremy Hunt were all in Toulouse already, so it must have something. Then Julian found the clincher – an international school built for all the British Aerospace people down there would be perfect for his son Oliver, pushing five. A recce trip settled it – Toulouse was the target.

Who was going to be in this all-conquering new team? The first answer was: not many. To maximise the budget available, we would be a single-programme outfit, with a tiny squad of nine or ten riders. Places from the existing team were going to be at a premium.

The existing team had in any case grown by one member. There were two main rival teams to Linda McCartney in the UK, Harrods and *Men's Health*. Both were run under peculiar arrangements that you wouldn't expect from household names. *Men's Health* magazine was not actually stumping up the small amount of cash that was covering their high-achieving squad. Instead it was coming from the people who were selling advertising space in the mag. Similarly, the money for the Harrods team wasn't plucked from Mohammed Al-Fayed's purse-strings, but was supplied by the man running the bike shop concession in the department store.

Harrods was the first to pop. Mid-season, not long after the Prutour, the team ceased to be a going concern when the money ran out, the man in charge disappeared and the riders were left high and dry and unpaid. We had long admired their star rider, the 1998 UK Champion

Matt Stephens, and to see him left without a team for the season seemed like a shame. He was drafted in immediately, grateful to be able to continue racing in what had been an excellent season up until then, with placings at virtually every major UK event. After a couple of Premier Calendar outings, where he was defending his overall lead in the season-long series, he was pleased to find himself off to the Tour Trans-Canada.

It could have worked out better for him, mind. On Stage Two, whilst sprinting across a small gap, his handlebar stem snapped in two, sending him crashing to the road in a very nasty accident. A broken collarbone meant a six-week lay-off and no opportunity to protect his lead in the Premier Calendar at home . . . circumstances had robbed Matt of a great year.

Plans continued apace for 2000. It was decided that there would be ten places available on the riding staff, with a star name wanted to lead our attempts to get into the big races. We were keen to emphasise and retain our British nature as much as possible, as we thought this was one of our strongest suits when looking for publicity and race invitations. We were determined to be seen as British, as vegetarian, as drug-free, as *different* to the other teams. Paul McCartney had even written a piece of music for us that you could hear every time you logged on to our website. Sampling a lyric from the old Beatles classic 'Penny Lane', Paul built a whole rave-type track around it and called it 'Clean Machine'. It was intended as our anthem, and what he would like us to be known as in the press. We were acutely aware that the worst thing that could happen to the team was a positive dope test . . . we would probably be better off never winning a race than having that happen. As a result, newcomers to the team had to be carefully vetted for past misdemeanours and made aware of their responsibilities.

A shortlist of potential British team leaders is always going to be just that: short. Of the current professional *peloton*, only three names were realistic targets. There was Chris Boardman, Credit Agricole's short distance time trial specialist and perennial Tour de France prologue winner; a household name due to his Barcelona Olympics success and still a real force in the sport as the World Hour Record Holder. There was David Millar, tipped as a future Tour de France winner, brimming with talent and in his early 20s, but still very much an unknown quantity. Then there was Max Sciandri, born in Derby to an Italian father before decamping to Tuscany whilst still in short trousers. He'd won big races for Carrera and then Motorola as an Italian rider, but continuing frustration with the national selectors for overlooking him for the Italian World Championship squad pushed him to take advantage of his dual nationality and become officially British.

Boardman was definitely of interest to us, as he was by far the best known among the great British unwashed, and would have guaranteed some good publicity. However, he had made it abundantly clear that he was only too ready to retire at the end of his current season with Credit Agricole, the only team he'd ever ridden for as a pro. Millar would be exciting indeed, and a great asset to the emerging force we hoped to be, but much was being made of his new four-year contract with Cofidis. To be honest, that seemed a better option for him anyway, steadily nurtured towards stardom in a well-established Tour de France squad. We could come back for him in a couple of years' time when we were massive. Sciandri was experienced, classy, always up there in the big races, week in, week out. He had the pedigree, the contacts, and he was looking for fresh challenges after a couple of years with the Francaise des Jeux squad. Surely he was our man.

Sean knew Max well from their days at Motorola, so he gave him a ring. He'd cost us around £200,000 a year, which is a few steps down the ladder in cycling terms. At the top there's Armstrong, hard to put a price on now, but pulling down about £3m at that time. Endorsements send his annual earnings high into the stratosphere. Plus, Armstrong is unofficially player/manager at US Postal; nobody is there without his say-so. In the next bracket at that time would come Bartoli, Ullrich, Cipollini, Museeuw, Jalabert and Pantani. They would all expect to get around the million mark, give or take a couple of hundred thousand. Then in the middle, you'd see classics winners and tour prospects like Bettini, Dekker, Tonkov, O'Grady or Vandenbroucke. There were plenty of riders as good as or more promising than Max who would be cheaper, but they wouldn't come with his *palmares* (CV of wins) or reputation. And they weren't British.

We made the offer he wanted and he signed, despite another offer from Mapei. He liked the idea of being the elder statesman and team captain, having some say in what was going on and helping the younger riders. He was very professional and the vegetarian approach gave him no problems whatsoever. I don't think there's any doubt that to ride with the McCartney signature on your back was seen to be very, very cool by a lot of continental riders, too.

We had our star . . . nine places left. David McKenzie had done more than anyone else to take the Linda McCartney team to the level we had already reached: he was a must. Chris Lillywhite was retiring but staying in the set-up. Chris Walker was keen to ride Premier Calendars again, but a full-on Euro programme seemed unlikely. Allan Iacuone had ridden brilliantly well in Malaysia, but had singularly failed to reproduce that form again. Frustratingly, that tantalising glimpse of class had looked more and more of a mirage as the season went on. Perhaps the vegetarian diet didn't suit him? Sean felt that he often looked bloated, though not fat; perhaps another team could get more out of him. He was reluctantly discarded, but remained a good friend. Matt Illingworth and Jonny Clay were committed to the GB track squad in Olympic year; they were unlikely to be able to play a full part even if they had been ripping up the road. They were to leave, and Matt given the option that there could be a place for him again in 2001 if he was still improving, and still wanted it. Julian Winn and Rob Reynolds-Jones had given everything for the team, but it was hard to see where they would find the extra 10 or 20 per cent they would need to make it abroad. Scott Guyton might have been an option if we were to pursue a Belgian programme, as he liked the windy flat roads and the bergs, but that was so far removed from the team's programme for 2000 as to be irrelevant. He was also sadly released with a promise to stay in touch for the future. Julian Clark was retiring to the desk full time, so that was one less body to count.

The potential stayers were Chris Newton, Ben Brooks, Matt Stephens and Russell Downing. In a 14-man team like the season before, they would have all been kept on, but we had a few queuing up to make such a small team in 2000. The Danish team Acceptcard were breaking up, and they had a number of tasty riders looking for work. After talking to Brian Holm, a contemporary of Sean's and now the Acceptcard DS, Sean plumped for Bjornar Vestol and Tayeb Braikia. Tayeb had missed most of the year after a terrible crash, but Brian recommended him as a seriously quick sprinter and a very professional rider. Bjornar would fill the Sean/Illingworth role of tireless workhorse with genuine class.

Sean had been tracking the Irishman Ciaran Power for the second half of the season. The Irish squad were often riding the same races as us, and Sean was impressed by the way Ciaran was always there or thereabouts no matter what sort of race it was. He'd finished 17th in the Prutour and he was only 23.

Max was asked if there were any riders he'd like to bring with him. The first was a surprise: we hadn't heard of Maurizio de Pasquale, an Italian from Amore e Vita who had turned out to have won a stage of that year's Tour of Switzerland. He was experienced, at 30, and Max thought he would add a bit of steel and know-how to what was looking a very young squad, so he was in. His second pick looked like a blinder: we all knew who Pascal Richard was. He'd cost a few bob, maybe £100,000, but blimey, this was the Olympic champion. If his name alone got us into a few races he would have paid his way. If he could come up with some rides from his glory years we'd all be laughing all the way to the podium. His best years were certainly behind him, but in those years he'd won any number of massive races . . . the Olympic Road Race, Liege–Bastogne–Liege, Tour of Lombardy, stages of the Tour, stages of the Giro . . . wow.

There was another interesting newcomer. Spencer Smith was somebody I had known vaguely since we were kids. He grew up in Isleworth, I grew up in Heston, but essentially we were both Hounslow boys. He was a swimming prodigy, one of those kids who got up at four o'clock in the morning to swim 50 miles before breakfast, fighting off a pervy coach in the showers every day. OK, so the last bit probably never happened, but that's what we always thought about those kids, wasn't it? No? You didn't go to my school, then.

By his teens, Spencer was one of Britain's best in the fledgling sport of triathlon. At 19, he was World Junior Champion. By the following year, he was World Champion proper, and retained it too, even though he was only 21 in a sport where supposedly you peaked after 30. All Spencer's victories were built around being first out of the water, crushing the opposition on the bike, then hanging on in the run. When the powers that be changed the rules to allow 'drafting', that is, riding close behind other riders during the bike leg, Spencer's chances of victory were slashed. As far as he was concerned, drafting was cheating, and triathlon was fast becoming a running race. Couple that belief with a seriously flawed positive nandrolone test that the authorities continued to hound him for, and you had a man totally fed up with his sport. Spencer knew Cel and Julian from the west London bike scene and he was good friends with big wheel and former pro Mick Bennett who also lived locally. Winter training for Cel, Julian, Spencer and me meant riding with the Sigma Sport boys on a Sunday morning from Kingston, and it was on one of those chilly November days around the Surrey lanes that a plan was formulated. Spencer was to give up triathlon completely and become a professional cyclist. For many years now, triathletes had often claimed to be fitter than cyclists, more up to date with training methods, more au fait with the benefits of new bicycle technology. Now, the triathlete who was best in the world on the bike would be racing against pro cyclists.

That was eight: Sciandri, McKenzie, Vestol, Braikia, Power, de Pasquale, Richard and Smith. Two spaces left.

Chris Newton had enjoyed a fantastic season against the clock. He had won the National 25-mile title, led a McCartney quartet to victory in the Team Time Trial Championship and taken the BCF TT Championship too, beating an in-form David Millar in the process. As a result, he was invited to represent GB at the Grand Prix des Nations, world cycling's most prestigious one-off time trial outside of the World Championships. Sean and Junior drove down to Forge-les-Eaux together for the race.

Sean always said that he would hate to keep any riders hanging on to find out whether they would have a ride for next year or not, as he and his teammates had been strung along so many times over the years. He thought it best to tell Junior as soon as possible that he didn't want him in the team for next year. It must have been an extremely quiet car journey.

'I couldn't really understand Chris Newton,' admits Sean now. 'I couldn't work out how he could get dropped in road races, then do such a great time trial. It didn't make sense to me. Take the Tour of Denmark. He gets spat on the first road stage, then runs Tyler Hamilton close in the time trial. If he was going to be a contender in stage races, he would have to get round the normal days as well as the specialist ones . . . it was all so frustrating.'

Junior would go on to prove Sean at least partially wrong by winning as hard a race as the Circuit des Mines in 2001, but his chances of becoming a top European pro probably evaporated with his place in the Linda McCartney team for 2000. It seemed a shame.

Keith Lambert thought so. He had been with Junior in one team or another for years, and had always rated him very highly. He thought that he would make a better addition to the team than the man Sean favoured, Matt Stephens. 'Matty was just better cut out for that sort of racing,' explained Sean. 'He might not have a sprint, and he might not be a top "tester", but he's got guts, determination, ability and he doesn't mind the long stages. He looks after himself brilliantly, climbs well, keeps his form right through the year and is an ideal teammate in a stage race.'

Stephens was in.

That left the two youngest riders, Ben and Russ. Keith was a big fan of Fonzie's and definitely thought he could make it in Europe, but was concerned that it might be too soon for him. 'I think he could do with another year,' he said. 'If we were running a bigger team, maybe, but with only ten riders, it's a lot to ask of him.' Although Ben was actually a year younger than Russ, he seemed a lot more sure of himself on the bike, and that streak of class had been noticeable throughout what had been a quiet year. We decided to take Ben to France and offer Fonzie the leader's role in the Under-23 team that would contest the Premier Calendar races with a view to joining the big boys in 2001. Everybody was very proud of Russ when he thanked us, but turned us down in favour of riding with an Italian Under-23 team instead, still with the intention of coming back in 2001. It showed the sort of attitude that Sean, Keith, Cel and Julian were looking for. Cel encapsulated it well, remembering his own early career: 'When I was 17 I could have gone to Belgium or anywhere, but I thought, "No, why should I leave me mates behind while I'm earning good money racing here?" Now I'll never know how good I might have been . . . I'm not saying I did the wrong thing, things worked out very well for me in Britain. It's just not knowing how far I could have gone that bugs me.'

So that was our ten for France. *Cycling* magazine slaughtered us for dropping the old guard, but it's unclear what else we could have done. Britain's best had patently not been good enough in 1999, to head into even more difficult battles with the same troops would have been Charge-of-the-Light-Brigade-ish to say the least. Our attempts to retain our national identity were ridiculed – 'Max Sciandri is as British as pasta' – and they made it clear that we would be considered no different from any other European team as far as their increasingly parochial coverage went. That was borne out when they reported the signing of Pascal Richard with a couple of meagre lines on their news page, whilst Gethin Butler's forthcoming attempt on the Land's End to John O'Groats record or a Saturday afternoon time trial on the A1 took precedence. That's not intended to belittle the performance and dedication of people like Gethin, just an indicator of where the country's best-selling cycling magazine's priorities lay.

Anyway, who cared what they said? We were going to the Giro d'Italia. We were going to Ghent–Wevelgem. We were going to the Tour Down Under. We were going to live in France!

Chapter 5: Coming Up

On 29 December 1999, Louise and I piled all our belongings into our 1974 VW Beetle and waved goodbye to my Mum and Dad. The car was so weighed down it looked as though I'd had it especially lowered for an evening of driving at 3 mph up and down Southend sea-front, Pete Tong rattling the hubcaps and baseball caps pulled tightly down over temples unburdened by Mensa IQs. We'd already kissed the dog goodbye – she was staying with our friends Andy and Sam Lyons in Leigh-on-Sea until we could get her new 'Passport for Pets' thing sorted out. My Mum had given us thermal underwear for Christmas, which was a nice touch, as it was bitterly cold and the heating didn't work in the Bug.

I'd already scoped out the Toulouse locale on a scouting trip with my friend Pete Clapp in the autumn, when Julian and Tracie were moving over there. Pete is known to all and sundry as 'Wilderness Man', due to his love of living in the woods off nuts and berries – those skills could have come in very useful as we explored the Foret du Bouconne that straddled the low ridge west of our home-to-be. Pete and I had been blown away by the whole place: the beauty of the rolling hills and villages of Gers, the buzz of downtown Toulouse and the majesty of the Pyrenees forever spiking the horizon wherever you were. By New Year's Eve, the Pyrenees were exactly where we found ourselves. A little gathering of friends made our way up to the pretty little ski station of Le Mourtis: there were Louise and myself, Julian and Tracie, the kids, Tracie's mum and dad, Spencer and Melissa, and their friend Rob. We had a fun afternoon kicking snow around and checking out cycling landmarks – Le Mourtis is at the top of the Col de Menté, where Luis Ocaña crashed and wrecked his chance of delivering Eddy Merckx's only Tour de France mauling. On the way up, we'd parked the Bug next to the Fabio Casartelli memorial to pay our respects to the man who had died on the descent of the Col de Portet d'Aspet.

On the way back to Toulouse, the Bug died. After a couple of years of sterling service, we had asked a little too much of her: a fully laden drive in atrocious weather all the way from England, followed by a tour of the Pyrenees in mid-winter were beyond her capabilities, and she began to make some extremely odd noises on the way back up the autoroute. I did my best to coax her back, but eventually she gave up the ghost about 20 km shy of our target. The engine seized up and died. It was 10 p.m. on Millennium Eve. It was beginning to sleet. The whole world was celebrating, and we were stuck in a lay-by in a foreign country with a dead car. This was a test for my French. I found a little emergency phone and bent into the mouthpiece, soaked to the bone with wind howling round me: '*Bonsoir, si vous plaît, aidez nous. Ma voiture, elle est morte!*'

We eventually crawled into bed exhausted in our rented granny flat just as the fireworks began to go off. Not the most auspicious of arrivals. I fell asleep troubled by a difficult question: when we first had duvets in England, they weren't called duvets, were they? They were 'continental quilts'. So how come, when I get to the continent, it's all sheets and blankets? Uurrrggghh, my brain hurts . . .

The rest of the New Year holiday was spent in Julian's new garage, me putting tyres on wheels, Louise sorting through pallets of energy food and muscle lotion. We only had a couple of days before Louise and the boys were off to Australia for some pre-season training leading up to the Tour Down Under, where I would join them for the race.

The pre-season in Australia was a great idea. Our small squad of ten could all go, with eight of them taking part in the race. From Australia, we were flying on to Malaysia and South Africa, so there would be plenty of opportunity for the two not racing in Adelaide, Spencer and

Ciaran, to ride. The team were billeted for two weeks in the homely surroundings of the Australian Institute of Sport's place at Henley Beach, a pleasant Adelaide suburb where you could walk out the front door of the old guesthouse, shuffle shoelessly across the road and straight on to the sand . . . beautiful. By the time I got there, the excellent team spirit and attitude were there for everyone to see. There were some seriously long training rides doing the rounds, including a speculative eight-hour monster in the South Australian heat. It hadn't started out as an eight-hour ride, but Sean had got lost. Asking Matt 'I-couldn't-find-my-way-out-of-a-paper-bag' Stephens to help with directions probably didn't aid his cause much.

There was a nice long winding hill out of the back of Adelaide towards the interior, and that's where we decided to get the team portraits shot. Sean drove slowly up the climb with Graham Watson, photographer to the stars, sitting in the estate part with the tailgate open and his frighteningly hairy shins hanging out the back. Why is it that bald fellers make up for it by covering the rest of their bodies in luxurious shag pile? The team rode gently up the climb in a group in front of the car, one by one peeling off to ride behind us for a few minutes of snapping.

When it was Spencer's turn, Sean said, 'Let's have a bit of fun, shall we?' As Spence began a game of thrust and counter-thrust with Graham ('Smile, can you?' 'I don't do smiling, it wrecks my image'), Sean gently slowed down until the other nine had virtually disappeared up the road. Having finished pulling his faces for the camera, Spencer suddenly realised he'd been had. He sprinted round the car, making a noise that began as a growl and ended in 'Bastaaaaaaaards!' before grinding his way back up to the boys. Quite brilliantly, as a footnote, when the pictures came through a few days later, we were all delighted to find out that Spencer's face pulling and posing had left him looking like he had a stuck-on head. I got a perfectly serious email from a Belgian fan months later, asking if Spencer had been unavailable for the photo-shoot, that being the reason we'd had to superimpose his head on another rider's body?

Spencer was continually at the forefront of all activity. Before going out on the bike in the morning, he would spend up to an hour in the bathroom, making sure everything was just right. 'What's the point of all that?' Chris Lillywhite would say. 'You're going to get sweaty and dirty in a minute.'

'Listen mate, some of us've got a bit more class about us, ain't we?' Spencer would reply. 'Some people wear a shirt and tie to work, some wear bike kit, it don't mean you can't look your best, all right?'

'Ponce.'

The race went very well. Macca rode strongly in the evening crit that kicked things off, and things got even better the following day when Matt Stephens got into the break that would shape the whole race. It wasn't part of the plan – Matt wasn't meant to be as advanced in his training as some of the other guys, but he had been attentive in the early stages, and when the move including defending champion and big favourite Stuart O'Grady went clear after only 12 km, Matt was there. They raced hard for an hour or so, building a big lead, and eventually, dissuaded by some stiff crosswinds, the bunch gave up the chase. Sean and I drove up behind the break to see if Matt was OK. He was blowing hard, but not at his limit, and Sean backed him to stay in there. 'Don't do too much work, Matt,' he warned, knowing Matt's tendency to punch more than his weight in smaller races. 'These boys are bigger names than you, let them do it.'

When you are in a break of 11, as Matt was that day, you can make a few enemies if you don't do your fair share of work on the front. The idea is that each man rides through to the front then pulls over smoothly, so you have a constantly rotating group comprising of two lines, one line moving past the other to take over at the front then sliding across to go back towards the back of the line. Problems start to begin when people try to miss turns by sliding to the back, then leaving a gap for the next rider to move into, rather than pushing through themselves. This leads to rows that can turn ugly. One way of beating the unpleasant practice is to fill the gap offered, then slow down, letting a new gap open. This is called 'taking someone out the back'. The miscreant is then forced to choose between sprinting past to close the gap down or losing his place in the break. The situation is further complicated if two or more riders from the same team get in a move. Other teams will then expect them to do more as a partnership than they would do individually, as they will be in by far the strongest position to take the win if the break reaches the finish intact.

On this occasion, the 11 breakaways rode smoothly together, each man tapping through gently and off, the speed remaining high. By the time they hit the streets of Goolwa, they had built up a gap of more than 26 minutes, far too much to be made up in a one-week stage race with no mountains.

It also made the race different for the team from now on. Having a man well placed overall gave the side a lot of focus: look after Matt, keep an eye on the other ten danger men, try to get into breaks, always look for a stage win. When the instruction is just to look for a stage win, it is easier to roll along without a great deal of purpose.

Matt was eventually an excellent eighth overall, a superb result and justification for Sean's insistence on getting Matt a place in the team.

The atmosphere at the Tour Down Under is relaxed to say the least. For a start, the whole race is stationed in the Adelaide Hilton for the week, so the accommodation is excellent, and there are no transfers to worry about. The weather is nice, the stages aren't too long, and the season proper in Europe won't be starting for another six weeks or so. The racing is serious, but there's time for enjoyment too. Pascal was keen on a night out whenever the opportunity came up. He was a surprise to all of us – a teenager stuck inside a 35-year-old's body, Mr Smooth with the ladies and often caught propping up the hotel bar with a pina colada late at night.

Perhaps this would be a good time to tell you about a couple of the more salacious stories I came across during my time with Linda McCartney . . .

DIRTY STORY NO. 1

We went to ride a French Cup race, GP Cholet, on the day after Milan–San Remo. One of our riders had brought a girlfriend with him, usually a total no-no, but allowed by Sean this time due to a special request. On the afternoon before the race, after arriving at our hotel, most of the guys went out for a training ride to turn their legs over after the journey. A Milan–San Remo game was on the box, so I stayed in to watch it. After the finish, I was looking for somebody to talk to about it, so I stuck my head out into the corridor to see who was still in and who had gone out. The door to the room next to mine was ajar, so I tapped on it and walked in, beginning to say, 'Did you see Milan–San Remo? What about–'

The words stuck in my throat as I was greeted by the sight of a man's shaven legs topped by a hairy arse, bouncing up and down upon the prone figure of a lady. I ran, closing the door after me.

DIRTY STORY NO. 2

Matt Stephens was chatting to another more experienced rider about the possibility of Linda McCartney getting a start at the Giro d'Italia. 'You'll like the Giro, I wore the pink jersey there last year,' said the old pro. Matt frowned – he'd watched the 1999 edition of the Giro fairly avidly and couldn't remember seeing this chap in the lead at any time. Seeing his confusion, our friend laughed, 'No, not *that* pink jersey. I won the real pink jersey. I slept with more girls than anyone else during the race.' This dodgy character, apparently happily married, claimed to have bedded 13 sadly deluded women over the course of three weeks' racing. And cycling's supposed to be exhausting enough.

DIRTY STORY NO. 3

Before my time, there was actually a World Cup race in England, called the Leeds Classic. That was the one time in the year that the big names would visit the UK, with big crowds of cycling nuts lining the roads over the Yorkshire hills. The night after this race, three old European pros went for a night out in the city, hooking up with three local girls who happened to be cycling fans. 'My one wasn't too bad,' my correspondent predictably claimed, 'but the other two were rough. (Rider No. 2)'s one was awful, and (Rider No. 3)'s had a twitch that meant she was constantly shaking her head.'

After a night of passion back at the hotel, the three met again over breakfast. 'We asked (Rider No. 3) what his night had been like. He said that by the morning, she wasn't shaking her head any more – she was nodding.'

Boys. What can you do?

DIRTY STORY NO. 4

At a big race later in the season, our part-time mechanic Gianni struck up a friendship with the rather stunning, statuesque girl representing one of the race sponsors. They arranged a romantic night out, and Gianni waited in his room for the phone to ring as prearranged. It didn't ring. The reason it didn't ring is that she spent the night in the room next door with one of the riders.

So don't believe what they tell you – it does go on. Very sordid. And if it's going to go on anywhere, it's going to go on at the Tour Down Under. The combination of good weather, a decent hotel, the long distance from home and less-than-pressurised racing means that the local girls are considered fair game. And Australian girls don't have a reputation for being difficult to get along with. I was safe – I was with my wife.

After Adelaide, we flew to Kuala Lumpur, then on to the island of Langkawi for the Tour of Langkawi. It's actually the Tour of Malaysia, but the gist of the race is to build tourist traffic for the budding resorts on Langkawi, hence the name.

Some of the boys had been here last year, Macca famously winning that stage, and Bjornar winning one too for his Acceptcard team. This was a six-rider race, so we shuffled the pack: Spencer and Ciaran would start their first race for Linda McCartney, with Matt, Ben, Macca and

Bjornar there too. Max, Pascal, Maurizio and Tayeb could go back to European training until a rendezvous in South Africa after Langkawi was done with.

Langkawi is a totally different race to Down Under. As I mentioned before, the mixture of experienced pros and South-east Asian composite squads make for interesting, if not downright dangerous racing. By way of an example, let me tell you about something that happened after a couple of stages.

The Chinese team were not the best, but they were in there and involved every day. On the particular day I'm thinking of, the bunch was all together as they approached the daily feed station. The feed is always a bit of a laugh. A *soigneur*, or sometimes two *soigneurs* depending on the number of riders in the team, will stand at the side of the road holding up *musettes*, little cotton bags in the shape of a satchel. There is one of these for each rider, and he snatches it from the *soigneur*, slips it over his shoulder and transfers the sandwiches, rolls, cakes, sweets and a can of Coke into his jersey pockets before dispensing with the bag by tying it into a ball and chucking it away.

That's what usually happens, anyway. On this day, there was a *soigneur* who was not fully concentrating, thinking all his riders had passed. There was a rider who was also not fully concentrating, and was on the wrong side of the bunch as his *soigneur* loomed near. He cut a quick swathe through the bunch, drawing a few irate Belgian swearwords, and headed for the dozing *soigneur*. Now, the accepted technique for taking a *musette* is to grab the straps with your hand before transferring it to your shoulder. Either nobody had told this chap, or he thought he'd be clever and put his hand straight through the straps and directly onto his shoulder. It might have worked if the *soigneur* had been paying attention, but as he wasn't, he neglected to let go of the bag, thus neatly lassoing the hapless rider clean out of his saddle, with a resounding *Enter the Dragon*-style 'Hooooooowwwwww!' He landed right on the flat of his arse.

'The funniest thing of all,' said the watching Matt Stephens, 'was that his bike carried on like a loose horse in the Grand National.' The riderless steed wobbled on past the bunch before dropping off into the ditch, while its rider hopped about in the centre of the road, clutching his bottom in pain.

'When we came round the corner a minute later, we couldn't figure out what was going on,' said Chris Lillywhite, accompanying Keith Lambert in team car 1 for the duration of the race. 'There was this Chinese bloke leaping up and down, jabbering and holding his bum, with no bike in sight. I thought he'd been stung by a bee.'

The whole team rode with tremendous bite and team spirit in Malaysia. Every stage finish would see McCartney jerseys at the front of the bunch, or riders trying their hands at late attacks. Bjornar in particular came close to recreating his '99 win on several occasions, but was always captured in the closing stages. Spencer was always looking to mix things up. His favourite trick was to attack the second that the flag went down to signify the start proper of each day's stage, which the Italians absolutely hated. They would be shouting, '*Piano, piano!*' to get him to slow down, but Spence would shout back, 'I don't play the fucking piano!' and ride off.

He was great fun off the bike too. Each night we would put Fifa 2000 on my laptop and become football stars, Spencer and Cel turning the hotel room into a stadium every evening.

There were some really tough stages, especially considering that we were racing at the end of January and into February. A 12-stage race will always be hard at that time of the year, but to include two high, high mountain finishes plus a 245 km epic through the jungle was extraordinarily testing. The stage up to Tanah Rata in the Cameron Highlands remains the longest climb I have ever been up. It wasn't particularly steep, and the race manual called it two climbs: one of 40 km, the other of 20 km. In reality, there was just a mile or so of flattish road between the two: effectively, it was one 60 km climb, 40 miles uphill through a rainforest, emerging into the tea fields at the top. On that stage the whole team rode well, but Macca and Bjornar were superb, both supposedly non-climbers, but both finishing in the top ten.

For much of the race, there were smiling, shouting faces lining the roads, young and old people, townspeople and another wild type of native, high in mountain shacks cheering the riders on. Schools would turn out waving flags, cute little Moslem boys and girls dressed in white, waving and screaming like mad. The epic 245 km stage from Mersing to Melaka wasn't like that at all – we hardly saw a soul all day, just jungle. There weren't even any turnings, the strip of tarmac just rolled on and on and on, there were no views due to the trees closing in on both sides. To make it worse, there was a massive smash at the finish. As the 60 kmh field approached the final shakedown, they had to negotiate a tricky left-hander, complicated by a traffic island. As the riders compressed into the small space available, there was a touch of wheels, a locking of handlebars, and no fewer than 30 riders met the road in a sickening cacophony of twisted metal, agonised cries and juddering bones. Ciaran Power, Bjornar Vestol and David McKenzie all came down in the bedlam, and as they picked gravel from their elbows, Ivan Quaranta was proving again that he was the fastest man in the race, taking his second win in as many days. Simultaneously, proving that cycling success is inexorably transient, the former yellow jersey Daniele Contrini was lying prone in a Melaka street with a broken collarbone and dislocated shoulder.

Quaranta and his team Mobilvetta were making few friends. It is the task of the sprinters' teams to keep the pace high towards the end of a stage, to chase down breakaways and to set things up for their fast men. Mario Cipollini's Saeco team were the masters of this right through the '90s, setting a standard for other teams to match. However, Mobilvetta made little attempt to do this. Knowing that Quaranta was the quickest, they let teams like McCartney, Bonjour and Farm Frites make all the running, do the donkey work, then up would pop Quaranta in the last few yards. There was nothing illegal about it, it just made them unpopular with the other teams, and didn't do them any favours. Sooner or later, the other teams might be needed to help you.

None of our boys were seriously hurt in the Melaka pile-up. When we watched it on video later, there was much hilarity as we saw that as soon as David McKenzie knew he was going down, he had rugby tackled Bjornar in an unconscious attempt to save himself.

The last of the monster stages was the crippling slopes of Genting, where Albie Iacuone had done so well a year ago. Going into the stage, Matt was in 19th, around two minutes off the lead. Chris Horner of Mercury had been leading for a few days, and his American squad had controlled things pretty well. We thought that we could put them under some pressure, though. The race wound out of Kuala Lumpur from under the Petronas Towers, then on to the mountain. Spencer attacked right at the bottom, a move designed to draw the hand of some of the other teams. As the pace quickened and the field began to thin down, Matt launched his big move. Matt Stephens is a good climber, but he lacks the change of pace that pure mountain goats like Marco Pantani possess, so it suits him to go early and set his own pace on the climb. He quickly destroyed the field, riding away from everybody. It began to split all over the place behind him, riders soon finding themselves in twos and threes. Mercury handled the situation well, keeping two teammates alongside Horner and letting him ride within himself to stay within the two minutes he needed to hold over Matt. At the top of the misty mountain I waited for the riders to come up, Cokes and towels at the ready for exhausted faces. The last timecheck we were given showed Matt a minute clear, but there was no news in the last few kilometres. I watched with Phil Liggett, the TV commentator and I straining to see who would be first around the last corner. When he finally arrived, it wasn't Matt: Perez, the Mexican climber from Panaria, was first. He'd caught Matt in the very last kilometre, as the road steepened over the last few hairpins. Matt collapsed over the line in tears and pain a few seconds later. 'I'm sorry,' was all he could say, which was enough to squeeze a couple of tears out of me too: he'd given everything for the team, and all he could think to do was apologise for not winning.

Perez went on to win two mountain stages in the 2002 Giro d'Italia and prove himself one of the world's finest climbers. To have beaten him that day would have been incredible, but Matt came within a hair's breadth of doing just that. He moved up to fourth overall – two big races completed, two top-ten places for Matt and Linda McCartney.

We left Kuala Lumpur with a slightly bad taste, as my laptop was stolen from the pressroom at the Hilton. I had done what every journo does at big races: find yourself a table, plug yourself in and spread your stuff out a bit to make it your own, then chin off somewhere. When I got back, it was gone. Spencer was gutted: 'How are we going to play football when they've stolen the stadium?'

South Africa began on a high:

MAURIZIO MAKES IT A LINDA McCARTNEY DAY TO REMEMBER

Maurizio de Pasquale of the Linda McCartney Pro Cycling Team scored a brilliant first victory for his new team when he took Stage Two of the Rapport Tour of South Africa today. There was double joy for the team when Olympic champion Pascal Richard made it a 1–2 for the Linda McCartney squad. The aggressive riding by Linda McCartney saw 'wunderkid' Jan Ullrich and his Telekom teammate Alberto Elli in particular take a terrible pasting. Elli was the overnight leader of the race, having won Saturday's opening stage. Today he paid dearly, as he was first left struggling by a blistering attack from McCartney's Max Sciandri, then flattened by the de Pasquale/Richard combination punch on the final climb to the line.

It was a difficult day, as the wind was blowing so hard on the coastal roads around the Cape that the stage was in danger of cancellation. It was also very hot, though the riders were not always fully aware of the temperature with the strong wind blowing across them. There were many casualties of the conditions, with dropped riders limping into the finish in ones and twos far behind the victorious McCartneys.

Max Sciandri and Pascal Richard featured when the race

began to hot up before the day's first climb. They initiated a dangerous break that caused panic among the ranks of Telekom riders behind. The break swelled to around 40 riders, with Sean Yates extremely pleased to see all six of his men making the split, the only manager who could make such a claim.

As the race crested the top of the hill, Max Sciandri launched one of his trademark attacks, striking out for the finish alone, with 40 km and three more big climbs to overcome. Behind, second-placed rider Tobias Steinhauser of Gerolsteiner sensed that Elli was struggling to stay in contention following Sciandri's escape. Steinhauser's team, spotting an opportunity to put the boot into Telekom, their German rivals, sent all their men to the front in pursuit of Max, with Elli in all sorts of trouble. The fierce coastal winds and the baking heat were beginning to take their toll on Max, and his brave effort finally came to an end as he turned on to the final 7 km climb to the line. But the whole Linda McCartney team were absolutely determined to get something out of the day, and Olympic champion Pascal Richard demonstrated his great winter training by blasting out of the bunch on the early slopes.

'Another guy tried to get across to Pascal, so I jumped on to his wheel,' explained Maurizio de Pasquale. 'He got about halfway across the gap and then "blew", so I jumped round him and on to Pascal on my own.' Their team strength had left Linda McCartney with two riders clear of the field in the last two km.

'Maurizio was going like an express train. It was marvellous,' said Pascal. 'I stayed with him for a little while, but he was going so well I shouted "go, go", to him and he went on his own to win.'

Maurizio celebrated in style at the finish, 14 seconds clear of Pascal and 22 seconds ahead of the rest. Linda McCartney had pulled off their first win of the season, and a flamboyant hilltop 1–2 at that. 1997 Tour de France winner Jan Ullrich was left floundering at nearly five minutes. The audacious attacking by Linda McCartney had given Gerolsteiner the springboard to crucify the German superstar's teammate Alberto Elli and place their own man Steinhauser in the leader's jersey.

Another spin-off from the day's wonderful spoils was still to come. Max Sciandri has moved to second in the King of the Mountains competition after his great ride had split the race wide open.

So, a first victory for 2000 then, and a very stylish one at that.

John Deering
Linda McCartney Pro Cycling Team

Maurizio went on to take another stage win, with Max grabbing one too. Max also landed the King of the Mountains jersey for his attacking riding.

It hadn't all been plain sailing, mind. One morning, when Sean was out on his bike as usual, a UCI official came looking for him. 'Sean wasn't around, so I spoke to him,' said Louise. 'He told me that somebody had tested positive and he needed to see Sean. I crapped myself.'

'Louise was very calm when I got back,' remembers Sean. 'She just told me that we had a problem and that I needed to see "the man" as soon as possible. It wasn't until I got over to his room that I realised how serious it was.'

One of the riders had tested positive for an abnormal testosterone level. Sean knew immediately that it would be Max, as he had proved over the course of many years that he had a naturally high testosterone level, which had been monitored, checked and validated by the UCI's medical people since their early days together at Motorola. The only problem was that Max had forgotten to bring his certificate with him to the race from Italy. He was only allowed to continue in the race after some frantic phone calling and faxing of documents confirmed his innocence. For another team, this would have merely been an inconvenience, but an episode like this could spell the end of the whole Linda McCartney team if we weren't careful. There was more trouble in South Africa, foiled by Louise, when a photo-journalist tried to picture the boys eating meat. As they sat around the hotel dinner table waiting for food to arrive, a waiter approached bearing a big silver salver of cold meats. He plonked it down in front of Max at exactly the same time as this photographer popped up ready to take a picture. Louise cottoned on to what was happening and quickly nipped in front of the scandalmonger to stop him taking his picture. She gave him a piece of her mind and he laughed it off, making it out to be a joke as the waiter removed the offending meat platter. It was, all in all, a good experience – a reminder that there were people out there who would love to stitch us up all in the name of a story and we had to be wary.

The vegetarian issue was a big one. I have always thought that it had a lot of positives: from a PR point of view for instance, it was a godsend. We were newsworthy wherever we went. 'Do you guys *really* never eat meat?' must have been a question we were asked thousands of times. And we really didn't. There were no hard and fast rules hanging over peoples' heads about exactly what diet they should follow, but the main bit was clear: don't eat meat. What they did behind closed doors was up to them, really, but we were all pretty used to not scoffing steaks and such and it didn't seem to be too much of a burden, even to a big oinker like me. Perversely, my only problems came when we *did* go out, especially in France. I never had meat in the house, but if we went to a restaurant in Toulouse, the food would usually be great, except for some sorry excuse of a vegetarian option propping up the bottom of *la carte*. The excellent Antidote hostelry in our local haunt of Pibrac actually changed their menu to include a few meat-free dishes and encourage our continued custom.

There were more pluses to our 'no meat please' stance. Being a small squad anyway, the vegetarian policy helped keep us a very close-knit bunch and definitely contributed to the fantastic team spirit that ran through the McCartney set-up in 2000. And you're a lot less likely to get sick when you're staying in ropy hotel after ropy hotel if you stay away from the meat. We ate pasta by the skip-load, which was fine in Italy, but not so great in France at times, especially in *le Nord*. It's not complicated, is it? Get the water very, very hot. Put the pasta in. Take it out again. Even I can manage that. Not 'Let's make that water fairly lukewarm, drop the pasta in at about six-ish, then it should be nicely stewed for dinner at eight'. Yummy.

Our first trip to Italy was a difficult one. Sean had got us an entry for Tirreno–Adriatico, which would feature a field as tough or perhaps even tougher than that which would contest the Giro in May. If we could impress in the eight-stage top-ranking race, we could get ourselves invited to the Giro d'Italia. But before we could start Tirreno, we were contracted to do two races in Sicily. It turned into an epic of logistics, especially for Louise, who was scooting from airport to airport trying to scrape up all the team. Craig got ill – really ill, and had to be hospitalised. Eddie was at his bedside while our little mechanic was throwing up and on a drip in a grotty Sicilian hospital, and it was decided to bring him home to Toulouse. Eddie flew back with him, leaving Louise with the team. Sean had drafted in some *soigneur* help in the shape of a little Italian fellow called Andrea, and we called up Adrian Timmis to give us a hand.

'I wanted Louise to take a rest,' explained Sean. 'She'd been to Australia, Malaysia and South Africa flat out, and she needed a break. But she was having none of it, and burst into tears when I suggested it. She took everything I was saying as a criticism, when all I really wanted was her at her best. She was a damned good *soigneur*, but she felt like she had to do *everything*, all the time. It was impossible to ask her to do anything different because she just got upset. In the end I just stayed out of her way.'

I drove down to Napoli from Toulouse with Adrian in our brand-new Renault Espace that we had been waiting for. When I met Louise, the effect was much the same as putting my head in a hot oven. All her frustrations and tensions over her difficulties were aimed at me and it became impossible for us to hold any sort of conversation whatsoever without it descending quickly into verbal abuse. It wasn't the most conducive atmosphere for team harmony, and the lads found the whole situation pretty embarrassing. One night, Max asked if Andrea could do his massage for a change, and Louise took it as a massive personal slight. She huffed and puffed, stormed around, then topped the night by throwing her wedding ring at me across the room. Something had to be done.

Southern Italy was beautiful. Beautiful, but mad. One morning, driving to the start in Aversa near Napoli, Pascal was sitting beside me in the passenger seat talking to his wife on the mobile as we passed heaps of rubbish and beckoning Somalian prostitutes at the side of the road. '*Oui, je suis en Italie, le sud,*' he told her. She must have asked him what it was like, as he replied, '*Comme Afrique.*'

At times it was indeed hard to believe that you were still in Europe, but when we climbed up into the spine of Italy, round Monte Casino and on towards Isernia it was impossible not to be charmed by the beauty and history of the place. The stage from Isernia climbed up and over a high snowy ridge before dropping down into Luco De Marsi, a stunning medieval town set in a bowl surrounded by snow-topped mountains. Breathtaking. That stage also proved the quality of the race, as the field raced up the long climb to the ridge at breakneck speed. 'It was so hard on that climb!' gasped Ciaran Power as all the team managed to finish comfortably in the bunch. 'It shows what a hard race this is, because they were going completely eyeballs-out up that mountain, but still nobody gets dropped! In the other races we've been doing, the field would have been split to smithereens.'

Ciaran had a fantastic race, always involved, and Pascal and Max were always dangerous. It was team policy to attack as much as possible in the final half hour of a stage, knowing that this was the time when the live TV coverage was on each day. We wanted to be noticed.

McCARTNEYS PRESS FOR GIRO START

'The team have acquitted themselves very well in terms of

media coverage,' reported general manager Julian Clark. 'The aggressive riding means the jersey is often on the screen, and the many lone attacks we've launched gives the TV people plenty to talk about.'

There has also been much speculation in the Italian press about the likelihood of seeing the Linda McCartney team on the start line of this May's Giro d'Italia.

'Journalists ask me all the time if we will be there, and I say "wait and see", but we are certainly trying to make it easy for the organisers to select us based on our performances,' said Max Sciandri. 'All the articles that have been appearing in the papers this week make me think that maybe we have got a snowball gathering momentum.'

David Cassani, the former teammate of both Max and Pascal Richard in the 1990s, is now the mainstay of Italian TV's blanket cycling coverage. He visited the team at their hotel in Isernia to wish them all the best, and congratulated all the riders for their persistence and aggression.

'It is good for TV to have a team that give you many things to speak about,' he explained. 'I hope the McCartney team will come to the Giro. The field at Tirreno–Adriatico is virtually as strong as a Giro, so I don't see why they cannot make it. This is an excellent test for them.'

John Deering
Linda McCartney Pro Cycling Team

We drove back to Toulouse knowing we had a job well done under our belts. Things weren't so good domestically for Louise and me though. I agreed that we should split up. Sean told Julian that he didn't want to go to another race with the pair of us, and that, frankly, he was having great difficulty communicating with Louise. The final upshot of the whole situation was that Louise went back to England. It was a terrible time for us, but now I think we both agree that it had to happen; things were just going from bad to worse between us. I sometimes wonder if we wasted two years of our lives by clinging on to our marriage when it was clearly over, but then I think again and decide that you have to try, *really* try to get through it. Otherwise, you will always wonder what might have been. Eventually, we had to face up to the facts: she didn't like me any more and I didn't care very much. Neither of us did anything terrible to the other one, and to this day we care about each other a great deal. At least we didn't have any kids to mess up . . . the dog got all the stick. Kit and Louise live happily in England now, and I get the opportunity to see them both once in a blue moon. Kit's put on a little bit of weight, like all chocolate Labradors seem to, but she's still got an unbelievable amount of energy. Louise recently came out of retirement to *soigneur* for the Sigma Sport team at the 2002 Lincoln Grand Prix. Seeing her handing up bottles to Matt Stephens like old times brought a lump to my throat.

Unbelievably, it wasn't the last of the team's *soigneur* problems, either. It was probably too much to ask Eddie to become head *soigneur* of a team so early in his career, and he didn't respond well to the pressure of the work and the travel. He became increasingly tired, morose and emotional before he too left the team before half the season was complete. A *soigneur's* life: too hard for many.

Julian swallowed his pride and brought Adrian back in full time. He was good company, a regular visitor at my house, and unflappable. I couldn't imagine him getting too stressed.

For the races that Sean didn't do, when he needed a break, the second team of Chris Lillywhite and John Deering would step in, or, as we would soon be calling ourselves, the bluffers. We would go into managers' meetings before races without the slightest clue of what was going on, but desperate to appear knowledgeable and au fait with proceedings. At the Tour du Vendée for instance, we took our places solemnly around the huge conference table in the town hall like all the other managers. We nodded when they nodded, mumbled when they did. When they picked up their race programmes to check some detail, so did we. If they scribbled notes, we would make a convincing doodle

in the margin. God, we were good. The only sticky moment at that
meeting came when someone called out 'Linda McCartney!' and they
all looked at us. It took a moment for us to realise that we had received
the good fortune of being drawn first out of the hat for the order of the
convoy the next morning, and would have the pleasure of a close-up
view of the racing.

During the race, we needed at one point to overtake the *peloton* to
get up to the break, where Ciaran was doing very well. It was tricky, the
race taking place on narrow lanes over countryside not dissimilar to the
Cotswolds. On a wider stretch, Cel pulled out and put his foot down,
having obtained permission to overtake from the race referee. We got
within a dozen or so riders of the front when the road narrowed. We
spent the next 10 km or so with two wheels on the grass verge, racing
along virtually in the middle of the bunch with riders cursing us
roundly. Every time the road opened out, we would catch up a couple
more places, only to drop back again when it narrowed. It was a hellish
20 minutes or so. Eventually, sitting bolt upright behind the wheel
with his tongue sticking out of the corner of his mouth, Cel got right
up near the front again. Surely, this time we would make it. Then,
suddenly but surely, the race route took us over a hump-backed bridge.
We shuddered to a halt at the side of the pack, the whole field of 170-
odd riders streaming past. Sheepishly, we regained our original spot.
Ciaran would have to look after himself.

Worse was to follow at the team meeting for Paris–Camembert. We
sat down all jolly with our fellow managers, shaking hands and
laughing with them, when the extremely nice Henrik Redant of Farm
Frites asked, 'Where have you been?' Cel had got the times wrong: the
meeting had already finished; that's why they were laughing. Doh! The
bluffers agreed to keep that particular faux pas to themselves.

On 1 April, Sean rang from England with the news we had all been
praying for; we had been selected for the Giro d'Italia. Joy unconfined.
We went into Toulouse to celebrate that night, and have an 'Up yours,
Robert Millar!' drink or two. The Scot, formerly a Tour de France King
of the Mountains and now writing for *Procycling,* had declared that we

had no chance of getting a ride in the Giro at the start of the year. We toasted him and thanked him for the extra motivation.

At the start of the year, it had been difficult to write effective programmes for all the team, as we only had ten riders. It had always been the plan to leave Ben out of the 9 if we made the Giro, as he was just turning 21, and it would be a big task for him in his first proper pro season. However, it looked as though we might be finding we had a problem elsewhere in the team.

Spencer was really struggling with the transition from triathlon to cycling. He had trained fabulously well in the winter, totally dedicating himself to the new discipline, and he was always the most fun man to have in your team. The trouble was that he just kept getting belted all the time. 'Spence can ride at 40 kmh all day, no problem,' reflected Ben Brooks. 'But if he has to ride at 30 kmh for an hour, then 45 kmh for 20 minutes, he's in trouble.' The change of pace, the reaction to what was going on around him just wasn't there. Spencer and Melissa weren't enjoying France much either: it was a big shock coming from their place in California or their house in Spain. Things didn't go well for Spencer at Ghent–Wevelgem, our only start in the spring classics that year. He found himself dropped by the bunch after just 30 km of the planned 214, before the race had even started in earnest.

He wasn't happy. 'All these blokes are cheating, what chance have I got if I'm not prepared to take drugs?' he asked. Of course, there are drugs in cycling, but it certainly wasn't as prevalent or omnipresent as Spencer was suggesting.

The camel's back was broken just a few days later at the Tour of North Holland. It wasn't as big a race as Ghent–Wevelgem, but it was still hard. Once again, Spence found himself distanced by everybody else early on. This time, however, there could be no discourse on how the winner was a cheat, because the winner was our very own Bjornar Vestol. Bjornar brilliantly soloed to victory after Spencer had spent much of the day in the team car. The game was up – he knew Bjornar was clean, and there was more to his problems than other people taking drugs.

Spencer came to see Julian shortly afterwards. A week or so before
our trip to Belgium and Holland, there had been some good news for
Spencer, when he was cleared for the third time over a dodgy positive
test for nandrolone dating back to '98. Spence was a well-known critic
of the triathlon powers-that-be, and it appeared to most outsiders that
he had been hounded over an extremely questionable test. Now they
had taken their case to the highest court in sport, the CAS, only to have
their argument thrown out again.

It left Spencer with a tempting possibility. He could go back to
triathlon and give up on his attempts to become a successful cyclist.

'I'm sure Spencer would have made it as a good pro if he'd have stuck
at it,' said Sean Yates. 'It would have taken him maybe a couple of years
though, and I doubt that he would have been a world champion or
Tour winner, but a good pro nevertheless. I just think that Spencer
wasn't used to not being much good at something. He'd been at the top
of his sport since he was a boy and now he was having to endure being
last. I don't think he expected to be winning races immediately, but he
wasn't ready to get hammered like he was.'

Spencer quit the team. He went back to triathlon, and went on to
become one of the world's finest Ironman triathletes.

We missed him though; missed him bad. He might not have won
much for us, but he was such a good bloke to have around. I felt bereft
without Spencer and Melissa around, and I miss them so much that
I've even been known to suffer the extreme boredom of going to watch
a triathlon if I know they're going to be there – now that's friendship.

Day in, day out, I have to listen to the latest crackpot training,
racing and preparation ideas that triathletes come up with. You'd think
they might recognise that cycling, having been around as a top sport
for well in excess of 100 years, might already have some fairly sure ideas
of what works, wouldn't you? No. Apparently we've been doing it
wrong. How kind of them to share all their new knowledge with us.
Much as I love Spencer, and enjoy his ridiculing of outlandish new
triathlon theory, when I hear a triathlete rubbishing cycling, I conjure
up the memory of Spence's tribulations at McCartney and smile sadly

to myself. He was the best cycling triathlete in the world, but sadly, he couldn't be the best cyclist.

We drafted in an American who had been recommended to us by Noel de Jonckeere in Belgium, a protégé of Chris Carmichael, Lance's coach.

His name was Matt De Canio, and he was a really good kid with a fantastic Armstrong-esque pedalling style. He wasn't used to racing long distances though: we tried him at the French Cup events like Paris–Camembert and the Tour de Vendee, where he was very keen and animated, but totally shagged out after 100 km. He was a great prospect, but he wasn't going to be able to tackle the Giro. Our team would be the nine survivors from the beginning of the season: Tayeb Braikia, Ben Brooks, Maurizio de Pasquale, David McKenzie, Ciaran Power, Pascal Richard, Max Sciandri, Matt Stephens and Bjornar Vestol.

Look out Italy.

Chapter 6: Bigger Than The Beatles

Seeing a dead person is bad. Being a dead person must be even worse, but seeing one is upsetting, even if you don't know them from Adam, or indeed Eve.

All the boys were negotiating the mean streets of downtown Rome a day before the big kick-off in the Tour of Italy when a young moped-borne local met an untimely and grisly fate at the business end of a Fiat. *Carabinieri* at the scene directed Pascal, Max, Ciaran and the other McCartney boys around and through the carnage with much furious whistle blowing and gesticulation, their narrow tyres picking up freshly shattered glass and glooping through a slick of leaking fuel. All around, horns echoed inanely and cold-heartedly, like a nightmarish crass recreation of *The Italian Job*, as tragic death and a terrible mess merely served as an irritation to the inflammable Romans. Italy: you couldn't invent the place.

Even for us, the morning's events were relegated to not much more than a distraction, because we had to get ourselves sorted for our audience with the Pope. Yep, that's right, the big feller, God's foreman, white hat and all that. We were *that* important. Everybody started stressing because we didn't have any smart matching suits or blazers like the other teams. We agreed that the management (represented by Sean, Cel and myself) would wear our groovy denim shirts, whilst all the riders would be in their tracksuits. Some thought this was fine, some found it funny, some a tad embarrassing . . . but one was mortified.

'Awww, *man*,' groaned Max with real feeling. 'I'm gonna meet the Pope looking like an English tourist.' Suspicion crossed my mind, as it often did with Max, that he was more concerned about what his peers in the other squads would think of him than offending the Pope's sartorial sensibilities.

'Don't worry, Maxi, you *are* an English tourist,' I nudged him, but without much of a response. At times like this, the dual-nationality Sciandri seems about as English as Zola Budd. Then when we gathered in the foyer of the Holiday Inn and checked out the assembled team and staff from Fassa Bortolo in their sharp Italian threads, I could feel the colour begin to rise in my cheeks, and wished I had been a bit more vehement in pushing for the team to provide some smart gear.

As the nine riders shuffled out to the bus, man-made fibres rustling enough to generate adequate electricity to power a small Christmas light display, thoughts turned to another interesting diversion along the way. Our bus wasn't just collecting the Fassa boys and us before heading off to see the representative of Heaven on Earth, we had to pop into the Sheraton Golf Hotel and pick up Mercatone Uno. This team were the focus of feverish media attention in the days leading up to the big start in Rome. In 1998, Marco Pantani, not only their leader, but the man whom the whole organisation was built around in the manner of the old-style European oligarchy teams, had flown to victory in both the Giro d'Italia and Tour de France. The tiny bald-headed *Pirata*, as he liked to be known, had used his undisputable climbing talents to utterly crush his rivals in the mountains and become a demi-god in Italy. His story was like a tale from a '50s boys' comic, full of eyebrow-raising nuggets: he weighed little more than 50 kg after going on a diet of nothing but popcorn; he started shaving his head because his premature baldness made him look like a veteran rather than the 22 year old he had really been in his first Tour in '95; he had come back from two life-threatening accidents; after his leg was shattered during Milan–Turin in '97 he wore a plastic bag pumped with air around it for six months; his whole team dyed their hair yellow to celebrate his fantastic passage into Paris in '98 – Pantani bleached his goatee.

In 1999, he was cruising to an even more comprehensive defeat of his rivals in the Giro d'Italia, easily scaling the enormous number of mountain passes littered along the route by the organisers to facilitate a popular Pantani victory, when dark disaster struck. On the morning of the penultimate stage, it was announced that Pantani had failed a blood test, and had been thrown out of the race. To a cycling public already disenchanted by the police raids and rider strikes of the 1998 Tour de France, it was almost too much to bear. The poignant twist of Pantani, the man who had carried his dignity and skill above the furore to take that tortured Tour, now cast as the villain, was not lost on his fans.

Italians turned their back on the fallen hero in their millions. A year passed with scarcely a sighting of the little man from Cesenatico, let alone a race to speak of, until now. A month ago, Pantani had said publicly that he would not only ride the Giro d'Italia, but he would win it and prove all the doubters wrong. Ridiculous, said the commentators, how can a man not race for a whole year and expect to even finish the Giro? Because he is the great Pantani, cried his public, swollen suddenly in numbers once more after 12 months without the charismatic climber.

Signor Castellano and his people at the Giro were naturally delighted. The *parcours* of the Giro was once again liberally sprinkled with huge mountains in the hope that *Il Pirata* would be able to regain control of 'his' race. Could it be true? Would Pantani show up?

'Not a chance,' said Sean as the bus chugged up the Autostrada. 'You never know with Pantani, though,' said Max. A nervous chatter in Italian and a little English buzzed around the bus as we shuddered to a halt outside the suitably pink walls of the Sheraton Golf Hotel. Would he appear? Pigs might fly, said some. Never say never, said the others.

Amidst the discussion, another small, charismatic figure who demanded respect in cycling rose to his feet from his seat near the front of the bus. A hush descended, as it was clear that Giancarlo Ferretti, manager of the Fassa Bortolo team, had something to say to all of us. He spoke with authority and belief to the upturned Linda McCartney and Fassa Bortolo faces like a mini-Italian Alex Ferguson, while Max quietly translated for the non-Italian speakers among us.

'You are all scared of Pantani,' began Ferretti. 'You are scared of a man who hasn't raced a bike for a year, whilst all of you have dedicated your lives to the next three weeks. Well, if he walks out of that hotel right now and gets on this bus, you had better stop being scared of him. Because if you remain in awe of him for the first week, letting him cruise along surrounded by a ring of teammates and ride himself into some sort of form, you will have been right to have feared him. Because then, when the mountains come, he will destroy all of you, and everybody will be laughing at you.'

Silence. Ferretti looked every rider in the face as the seconds passed. When he began to speak again, it was quieter, but with a burning intent.

'Pantani is a fool if he thinks he can come here and arrogantly dismiss us. Attack Pantani. Attack him all the time. Make him suffer. Let us see him grimacing every day at the back of the field. When we reach the mountains, Pantani will be finished.'

Nobody in cycling would suggest that Ferretti is not worth listening to. Moreover, few of us ever get the chance to hear him, and a murmur of approval and respect ran around the coach. Then everybody turned to our side of the bus to look out of the window as thin men in grey suits began to file out of the Sheraton. The Italians stood and leant across the aisle on our seats, craning their necks. A gasp went up as a shaven head appeared in the shadows of the foyer, then dissolved into nervous giggles as Stefano Garzelli, Pantani's similarly shorn lieutenant, stepped into the light. That looked like everyone. Except that, amongst the managers, *soigneurs* and hotel staff, we could only see eight riders. Then suddenly, he was there, on the step, alone, eyes protected from the glare of the sun and 30 piercing stares by a pair of cool Italian shades. Hands in his pockets, looking every inch the returning hero, Pantani sauntered down the steps, joined his teammates and clambered on to the bus.

A dozen '*Ciao Marco*'s and a liberal sprinkling of macho handshakes later, he settled into a seat directly behind Matt and I near the back, every inch the playground tough guy. I half expected him to light up a rebellious Marlboro. The two residents of 13 Lot du Castelets, Aussonne raised a silent eyebrow at each other before focusing on another mad police-escorted dash through the mean streets of Rome.

Bathed in glorious May sunshine, a couple of hundred cyclists, *directeurs sportifs*, flunkies and even the odd press officer tumbled out of a wheezing array of old coaches into the magisterial surrounds of the Vatican. Sean called me over to where he was chatting to a slight-looking guy with curly hair, jeans and a rucksack, looking every inch the amiable tourist. 'John, this is Andy Hampsten,' said the boss, as I proffered a quivering hand to the winner of this very race in 1988. 'Hey there, Jarrn Deering, right?' 'Err, yes, your worship, I mean Andy, I mean Mr Hampsten,' I mumbled, taken back at just how damn *nice* this guy was. I gathered my wits enough to engage in conversation with the now retired American who had been Sean's team leader at 7-Eleven and Motorola. Now living idyllically in Tuscany running holidays for visitors from the States, but still looking amazingly fit, Andy was an invitee to the Pope's tea party as a previous Giro winner. Five minutes' chat was enough to leave me with a lasting impression of a man at peace with the world and nothing to prove to anyone. No wonder Sean thought the world of him. I had strangely been rendered star-struck by one of the smallest egos in cycling.

Not that there was a shortage of stars chattering and enjoying the sun in Vatican Square. Alongside current stars like Pantani, Mario Cipollini and reigning champion Ivan Gotti were Andy Hampsten's fellow former winners: Felice Gimondi, Stephen Roche, Francesco Moser, even the legendary Eddy Merckx. A cycling giant whose imperious shadow is still cast long over the sport 25 years after his retirement, Merckx is now a giant in form too – years of abstinence have been replaced by a taste for the good life well earned. American journalist Andy Hood once told me about a man who gets up to the gates of Heaven to be met by St Peter. 'Peter says to the guy, "OK buddy, here's your harp, here's your little cloud, go and have a look around and just shout if you've got any questions." So he travels around for a day or two, checking out the great and good of days gone by frolicking in Sylvanian fields and generally enjoying the ambience of paradise just as he'd pictured it. Then, to his surprise and delight, he comes across a magnificent velodrome. He pushes through the unguarded turnstiles into an arena deserted save for a big old feller with a beard whizzing round the track hunched over the handlebars. When our man gets back to St Peter, he asks him who the cyclist is. "Oh, him," says Peter, tutting and shaking his head. "That's God. Thinks he's Eddy Merckx.'''

Inside the palace itself the childish and laddish cyclists' demeanour is held in check for once by the incredible architecture, history and good old-fashioned holiness of the place. We are shuffled into a room with the most incredible vaulted ceiling depicting the glorious passage of Pope Clement, and left to contemplate it for an hour or so, bony cyclists' backsides becoming uncomfortable on hard wooden chairs long before there's any sign of action. Our boys are more subdued than most, the tracksuits seeming more ridiculous than ever alongside the yards of beautifully cut Italian cloth hanging off everybody else crammed into the little chapel. I look down at my Linda McCartney denim shirt and am plagued once more by a childhood memory of a cheesy Christmas advert: a woman's sluttish nail-varnished hand caresses a hunky chest clad in a denim shirt whilst an Orson Welles soundalike drawls, 'Denim – for the man who doesn't have to try too hard.' Good grief.

As the silent minutes ticked by, I am prepared to wager that mine was not the only guilty mind wondering if some incident had befallen his Holiness. After all, JP2 hadn't been in the best of shape for some time, locked into a last-man-standing battle with the Queen Mother over beatific longevity. But then the enormous oak doors swung open and a whole bunch of cardinals breezed in, a man in white seemingly impossibly doubled over in a gravity-defying crouch in their midst. That was him, I reckon. We couldn't see much from the cheap seats.

Breaking through the excited multi-lingual chatter and creating an instant hush, an authoritative voice speaking Latin rang out via the ropy tannoy. Cel and I were impressed instantly by the old man's composure and strength . . . but then, between the dozens of rows of heads between us and the front, I caught sight of a chap in a suit talking into a mic, and realised that it was his voice we were listening to. Then, to a great murmur, he was up! On the move! And then down again. It was definitely him, though, I saw the top of his white hat. Unmistakable. There was more Latin, a bit of chanting including the parts we were meant to join in with, which led to some solemn nonsense-mumbling from the embarrassed English-speaking infidels in the McCartney ranks, then the man himself was helped to his feet and met with all the great luminaries in turn. A wave of unconfined joy swept through the rank-and-file cyclists as God's goalkeeper blessed their betters. Cel was so desperate to get a look, he stood on his chair, only to be talked down by Swiss Guards desperate for action after centuries of purely ceremonial duties.

I do apologise if my approach seems a little blasphemous. My ambivalence towards the Catholic Church is the product of my own upbringing in a long-lapsed Catholic family. My Dad, left distinctly unimpressed by his own Catholic schooling, politely declined our local priest's invitation to send your infant author to our neighbourhood Catholic school. Politely, that was, until the man with the dog collar opined that my folks would be crazy to send me to the local school because it was 'full of Pakis'. That's when Dad chucked him out into the street and told him to fuck off.

So I saw my role as more of an interested observer than a devotee, but I must say that it is impossible not to be touched by the genuine love and wonder shown by men I hadn't previously regarded as particularly pious. Heavenly photocalls complete, it was a genuinely joyous bunch who made their way back into the temporal world.

The prologue was scheduled for an extremely popular lunchtime start. It began on the stretch of avenue between the Colosseum and Mussolini's great white palace. After a morning entertaining the likeable David Sharp from *Procycling,* which involved him posing alongside a succession of locals dressed as centurions, we headed to the start area. Beating a way through a throng of fans desperately trying to blag their way through the temporary fenced compound, it dawned on me how big this thing was, and how much earth we had moved just to be there at the start.

Awaiting his start time, Matt Stephens sat calmly on the back of the start gate podium. We sat together for a minute, grinning in silence.

'It's really happening, isn't it John?'

Yes, it was really happening.

My only action was to chop up my own Velcro watchstrap for Bjornar's benefit, as the big feller's Viking chin was too broad to fit under the retaining strap of his time trial helmet. He roared off on the 4.6 km to the Vatican with a bit of my watch holding his hat down.

As the riders fired off one-by-one across the cobbles, I spotted a famous face leaning on the barriers next to me. Please allow me to digress slightly here. Trust me, it's funny. When I first got interested in cycling, my friend Neil used to say to me, 'Who do you think you are, Joop Zoetemelk?' You may think that a former World Champion and runner-up in the Tour may not be the first cyclist to spring to mind for those without a passing interest in the sport. Neil's familiarity with the Dutch maestro didn't come directly through cycling, however. Apparently, Joop had been a competitor on *Superstars*, every '70s schoolboy's favourite programme. Famously, according to Neil, Joop had managed a grand total of one push-up on the parallel bars – you know, the thing that Brian Jacks used to do about 100 times without taking a breath. It was the most pathetic performance in a long list of pathetic performances gracing *Superstars* over the years – Kevin Keegan falling off the bike, David Hemery falling in the water jump, various idiots falling out of canoes, that sort of thing.

And now here he was, the great *Superstar* himself, working for the Dutch Rabobank team and catching some rays on the barriers. I introduced myself to Joop and we had a short, smiling conversation in the Roman sunshine in stuttering French. After the pleasantries, I launched straight into it:

'My friends remember you from *Superstars*.'

'Ah yes, *Superstars*, that was a great honour to be invited.'

'They told me that you only did one push-up on the parallel bars.'

In a second, the smiling, genial Dutchman was replaced by a snarling, competitive dog.

'I was injured from the day before! They made me do it! I have never been so humiliated!'

With that he stalked off to perform some pressing team duty. I, on the other hand, grabbed my mobile and tapped in Neil's number:

'You will NOT BELIEVE who I've just been talking to!'

I hopped into the team car beside Sean to follow Ben around the course. He rocketed out of the start gate and bounced across the cobbles, the enormous Saturday afternoon crowd roaring him on. The course was incredible: instead of the wide boulevards often favoured by time trial course architects, this one took in the back streets of Rome, some little more than alleyways. I half expected Ben to race round a corner and be confronted by a washing line draped with drying white sheets. On the TV at the finish later I saw both Mario Cipollini and Paolo Savoldelli come nail-bitingly close to ending their rides in a heap next to uncomfortably placed brick walls. There was a liberal helping of cobbles, and so many corners that it was impossible to find a true time-triallist's rhythm. Suddenly, we rounded a corner and we were in a long straight with the Vatican filling the middle distance, the sun beginning to slide down behind it. Breathtaking. Ben pushed on to the line – afterwards he seemed subdued, and his time was a poor one. I would find out more tomorrow.

Without a prologue specialist in the team, the main aim for Sean was to finish all our riders safely. Max was the best, a respectable 30th, with Tayeb and Pascal close behind. Max and Pascal both drew great receptions from the crowd, always happy to cheer faces they recognised. The reaction was nothing to that given to the little baldie from Cesenatico though. When Pantani sailed round the corner at the bottom of the straight and began the drag up to the Vatican, the cheers were loud enough to have blown the old place down. Despite his pedestrian time, some 30 seconds behind Jan Hruska and Savoldelli, there was no doubting who was the boss as far as the fans were concerned – Pantani was back and they loved him for it.

The main thing on my mind on the morning of the first road stage was the question of Pascal's jersey. In cycling, a tradition has developed over the decades where riders who achieve something special can display their pride by wearing jerseys to denote their feat. This practice began many years ago, when the leader of the Tour de France wore the fabled yellow jersey each day so that the hordes stretched along the muddy roadsides might have a chance of picking him out as the bunch flashed by. Incidentally, that is why Pantani's Mercatone Uno boys don't wear yellow in the Tour de France – they switch to shocking pink to avoid confusion with the wearer of the *maillot jaune*. Then, after the inception of the World Championship Road Race, the winner wore a white jersey emblazoned with the rainbow hoops that would tell the public that this man was indeed the champion of the world, and would wear those colours in every race for the whole of his year-long tenure of the title. That spread to national champions too, so that some of Bernard Hinault's greatest victories, for instance, were achieved in the *tricouleur* jersey of Campion de France.

In 1996, the Atlanta Olympic Road Race took on a huge significance to dwarf all previous occasions. Now that the Olympics had been thrown open to all sportsmen, the race could be contested by professionals for the first time. Until then, the Olympics were regarded by cycling fans and cognoscenti as merely a good pointer as to which junior riders might go on to become genuine stars in the 'real' races. So it was that the field lined up in Atlanta was one of the most star-studded in history. The great Miguel Indurain was about to make his final bow whilst still very much at his peak, the pre-cancer Lance Armstrong was on home territory, Tour de France champion Bjarne Riis still had points to prove. Yet it was an experienced trio of cycling's best one-day riders who took the day from the favourites. Denmark's Rolf Sorensen, Switzerland's Pascal Richard and Great Britain's Max Sciandri stole a commanding lead from the rest and worked hard enough to ensure that they would decide the order of the medals between themselves. Sciandri, on paper the best sprinter, was exhausted and had been a virtual passenger for the last few miles of their mammoth breakaway. He led out the sprint early, setting up his two companions for a desperate dash to the line. Cool to the very last second, Pascal would not be shifted from Sorensen's wheel. Both winners of the great Liege–Bastogne–Liege classic, each man knew that there is more to sprinting at this level than being the quickest in a straight line – to be the cleverest is to be the winner. With the enormous crowd bellowing in his ears, Pascal summoned all his strength for one burst of speed that carried him past the Dane to become Olympic champion. Max rolled over the line a couple of seconds later to take a famous bronze for Great Britain.

Pascal really knew how to make the most of his fame. Already one of Switzerland's best-known sportsmen thanks to an incredible string of results over the years, boyish good looks and a playboy reputation, he now put the medal to work for him. Now, when asked for his autograph, he would add a little five-ring Olympic motif and a '96' to his signature. San Marco made an 'Olympic Champion' signature series saddle for him, also bearing the rings. Most of all, he joined the club of cycling champions by having the Olympic rings incorporated into the design of his team jersey. He was a great asset to any team wishing to draw attention to themselves, and knew he would be carrying the title right through to 2000, unlike the world champions, impoverished by comparison, who only had a year each to parade their rainbow jerseys.

When the Linda McCartney team picked up Pascal in the close season between 1999 and 2000, it was largely in the belief that his visibility in what would be an Olympic year would pay dividends to a smaller team trying to make a name for themselves. Principia, our Danish bike supplier, made Pascal's two race bikes in white instead of the team yellow, printing 'Olympic champion' along the top tube. We began immediately to have a special jersey designed that would tell the world that the Olympic champion was a Linda McCartney rider. However, we soon ran into problems. The UCI, cycling's governing body, sanctioned and ran the World Championships, but they didn't run the Olympics. The IOC, unused to the vagaries of cycling, objected to their trademark being used so freely, especially when they charged companies such as McDonald's or Coca-Cola enormous amounts to use the rings and call themselves partners of the Olympics. How could we, upstart Englishmen, expect to just take it to promote our company?

We were in our turn frustrated by the unfairness of the situation. Hadn't Pascal worn such a jersey for the past three seasons, firstly with Casino and then with Mobilvetta? Ah yes, they replied, but that's just because he's ignored us up to now; it's Olympic year and we're going to put our house in order. What about Paola Pezzo, the Olympic mountain bike champion? She always makes the most of those five rings. Ah yes, they sagely nodded again; we're on to her too. Even now, six years after Atlanta and with another Olympic gold on her dressing table, Pezzo is always but *always* dressed in a kit that tells the world she is the Olympic champion.

Julian came up with a compromise idea. If the issue with the IOC was linking a commercial company's name with the rings, let's design a jersey with the rings on, but without the McCartney logo. We'll do it in the same style and Pascal will still wear the normal shorts. We went ahead and had it made by Giordana, our kit supplier. It was a really special piece of kit: white, with the v-shaped red and blue of the normal McCartney jersey, and where the sponsor's logo should have been, those five coloured rings.

It arrived well before the Giro, and naturally Pascal wanted to wear it at once. He wore it when training in Switzerland, and intended to wear it in the last big test before the Giro, the Tour of Romandie, his local race, one that he had won twice in the past. But they were on to us. We got an email from the UCI back in Toulouse promising a hefty fine if he raced in a jersey bearing the rings, company name or no company name.

Frustrated and angered by the unfairness of the situation, Julian and I hatched a plan to push ahead with the jersey – but to ensure maximum publicity for when it did finally get worn.

'Even if we *win* the bloody Giro, it won't create massive shockwaves in Britain,' said Julian. 'The only thing that gets people at home interested in cycling is the Olympics. Look at Chris Boardman – there's no way that he would claim that the Olympic Pursuit gold medal was the pinnacle of his career. He's got to be more pleased with all those Tour de France prologue wins, those days in the yellow jersey, and the World Hour Record. Yet what does Joe Public in England remember him for? Barcelona Olympics, when he was an amateur.'

'So,' I projected, 'we want to get maximum exposure when we finally do get it on his back, then we'll wear the fine as money well spent.'

'Exactly. And we'll kick up such a fuss that the publicity will run and run anyway.'

So it was decided that the first stage of the Giro would see the unveiling of the jersey. We got Pascal to reluctantly wait until then by promising we would pay any ensuing fine – if he wore it on another occasion, it was down to him.

The sports papers in Italy were onto him and us. Pier Bergonzi from *La Gazzetta Dello Sport* asked me about it; Pascal was fond of training in the top if he couldn't race in it. I told Pier about our line of no-company-name-no-problem. They ran an article, and got some quotes from the suits at the UCI: 'It isn't allowed. If he wears it, he will be fined.' The tone of the articles was very supportive to us; after all, he'd worn the thing for three years and people had got used to it. It did seem a bit unfair to stop us now.

Little did I know that as I lay awake in the small hours in the Holiday Inn, these questions that had taxed me for months were about to be rendered completely irrelevant.

I thought I was up pretty early that morning, but when I got downstairs, there was already a huddle of worried-looking men in the foyer. Sean, Julian, the team doctor Roger Palfreeman and our Italian agent Pier Pieroni were in conversation. Julian beckoned me over.

'We've got a crisis,' he told me quietly and calmly.

The night before last, before the prologue, Roger had been doing all the final tests on the riders to check they were in the best shape and that nobody was going to trouble the dope testers.

In Pascal's room, during the course of getting some (it must be said) totally unremarkable results, Roger noticed a tub of some muscle-building powder on the bedside cabinet.

'What's this?' he asked Pascal, picking up the container for a look.

'Oh, that's some stuff I got from my gym, it's great,' said the champ.

To his horror, Roger saw that the 'great stuff' contained a substance that is quite clearly banned by the UCI, and would produce a positive test should Pascal get pulled up at some stage over the next three weeks.

'Jesus Christ, Pascal, how long have you been taking this shit?'

'I've had it for a few years, I've been using that tub since Romandie.'

'If you get tested, you're screwed.'

'No way, it's fine, the guy who gave it to me told me it's all OK.'

It was at about this point that the mild-mannered little doctor lost his rag.

'Fine? *OK?* This guy, he's a doctor, is he? A professional cycling doctor with a deep knowledge of the UCI's banned substances list? Jesus Christ . . . have you given any of this to anybody else?'

Pascal, totally shocked by the revelation, took a moment before replying. 'Ben has had some. He was nervous about being in such a big race for the first time, and I told him that this would make him feel stronger.'

Roger fumed out of the room and went in to see Ben Brooks. At 21, Ben was one of the youngest riders in the whole field. This fact alone would ensure plenty of media attention over the next three weeks – the dark, boyish good looks were a definite bonus as far as press coverage was concerned. He'd also become a good friend over the time we'd spent in Toulouse.

It was true. Ben had taken some of Pascal's magic potion.

'Shit, that was the worst night of my entire life,' remembers Ben now, shaking his head and fighting back tears. 'I'd had a pretty rough time of it that spring, but gone to Romandie with some good form after training my tits off in Toulouse. I was going as well as at any time since I'd joined the team; getting in moves, helping set up the sprints for Tayeb, looking after Pascal in the bunch. I was rooming with Pascal for the first time, and he was pretty helpful with tips and looking after me – I was only 21 after all, in my first really big race.

'I got in a break with Peron and some other hitters on one day, and was completely shafted by the evening. Pascal said he had some good recovery stuff that he'd got from his gym. I'm always worried about taking anything I'm not sure about, but he told me he'd been taking it for a few years, and it was all 100 per cent natural ingredients so I gave it a nudge. What an idiot . . . I can still hardly believe it now.'

'So what's the plan then?' I asked Julian in the foyer, the gravity of the situation sinking in.

'I'm pulling them out,' he frowned. 'I just can't risk it. You know that one positive test and this team is finished. It's bad news for everybody, especially for them, but I can't put everybody's jobs on the line.'

Pascal was livid. He defended himself by backing up what he'd told Ben a week or two before – he said he'd been using a completely natural recovery aid for a few years, during which time he had been dope tested countless times with absolutely no problems. At the start of what was likely to be the last major tour of a glittering career, the man whose riding had done more than anybody else to get us there was about to lose his place on the start grid.

The injustice of facing removal from the race was simply too much for Ben.

'I've never felt under pressure to use illegal stuff, and never felt the need to either. At the tests we had done I'd been told I had a naturally high haematocrit level anyway, so there would never be any point in taking EPO which was the big thing then, so I didn't even consider taking any gear. I was 21 – what would have been the point?'

I remembered a chat I'd had with Sean and his old team doctor Max Testa back at Tirreno. Testa, by then running the Mapei Institute for young riders, agreed that young riders taking illegal substances was bad for everybody, including the team, even if they were getting good results and not getting caught. He and Sean were of the view that you need to know what a rider is really like when he's learning his way in the sport – what's the point of signing and investing in a prospect if the only reason he's getting results is the medication plan he's following? Another believer in the clean approach was Ciaran Power, who echoed Ben's view: 'What's the point in me taking drugs? I'm 23 . . . if I start cheating, I'll never know how good I might have been.' It's a pragmatic and admirable stance that I wholly agreed with, and still do. It's essential to give riders a good reason not to take drugs. 'Just say no' is, quite frankly, insufficient.

Roger warned that Pascal and Ben could test positive for six weeks after taking the powder. Ben was allowed to return to Australia to get over his traumatic disappointment, but ordered to start the Under-26 race in Spain, where we were sending a team immediately after the Giro.

He refused, reasoning that if he could fail a test in the Giro, he could fail one in Spain too.

'Looking back, I marked my card with the team there and then,' he says ruefully. 'I was out of favour for refusing to start Circuito Montanes – they thought I just wanted to doss around in New South Wales, but it seemed like a crazy thing to do to me. Miss the biggest race I might ever do in case I tested positive for something that I had no inkling about, then run exactly the same risk at some bullshit little race that nobody's ever heard of? Where's the sense in that? I was no cheat, but I knew it wouldn't be seen like that. My career could have been finished before it had really started.

'As soon as I said that I wouldn't ride in Spain, it became clear that I would have had to do something pretty special to keep my place in 2001.'

And so began the Day From Hell.

The press release I sent out that night was euphemistic at best:

TOP TEN FOR TAYEB MASKS McCARTNEY TEARS

Tayeb Braikia of the Linda McCartney Pro Cycling Team used his flying sprint to take a great 8th place in the first stage of the Giro d'Italia, but the overwhelming emotion of the day was one of great sadness.

Both Ben Brooks and Pascal Richard fell ill after the prologue, and after a restless night, the pair were deemed unfit to start the first stage after being examined by the team doctor, Roger Palfreeman.

'It's hard to take in,' admitted team manager Sean Yates. 'We arrived here with nine riders at the top of their form, and we find ourselves going into the first stage with only seven men. That said, the boys really pulled together and rode very well indeed today.'

John Deering
Linda McCartney Pro Cycling Team

The bad press we expected didn't materialise. The story of Pascal's jersey that they had been waiting to write took the place of any supposed illegal substance-abuse conspiracy theories: apparently, our official line that Pascal was sick was designed to mask a massive bust-up between the champ and the team hierarchy, where he had been told in no uncertain terms that he would not be permitted to wear his treasured Olympic jersey. In a fit of pique he had refused to start, thus forcing us to fabricate a story about his illness. Brilliant. Except of course that there was no mention of Ben in this . . . perhaps he had been so close to Pascal that he wouldn't go on without him? It was all very silly, but served us well. Smiling, I denied all my fellow pressroom inhabitants' theories, secretly pleased that nobody had tumbled the real issues involved.

By the time the decision had been taken on the Rome Two, the truck, driven by Adrian Timmis, had already left for the finish in Terracina, 100 miles or so south of the capital. My new job for the day was to chase after it in my newly hired Fiat Ducato, get Ben and Pascal's cases, drive back to the Holiday Inn, take them to the airport, then drive back again to Terracina. Bad news for David Sharp, who I put in the team car with an understandably reticent and thundery Sean Yates. He was flying out of Rome that night, and I now had no idea how we were going to get him to the airport.

I found our lovely seaside hotel after a long drive, got the boys' stuff from Ada and began to head back. The return journey was not quite as easy though – the direct road was the race route, so I couldn't go that way, towards the oncoming race. Consulting the map, I wound up some little roads away from the coast and into the small mountains that characterise so much of Italy. It must have been at about this time that the turbo blew on my van.

It was early evening by the time I got back to Rome, sweating and miserable after driving the whole way back at about 30 mph.

Poor Ben was distraught. Having a day on his own to think about what had happened had left him a wreck, full of self-doubt and anger at himself. I reasoned that there would be plenty more opportunities for a man of his age, but I knew I wasn't helping much.

I dropped Ben off at the airport and picked up a new van. On the long night drive back to Terracina I considered the day's events. One day down, two riders down, and our first objective already scuppered: it would have been good to get all nine to Milan. What next?

Chapter 7: The Frog Chorus

Sean was right about the first stage: the boys had ridden well, Tayeb getting up there in the gallop, well supported by Max and Ciaran. Some lively interventions over the closing kilometres showed that we could hold our own in a race of this size and class. We, or at least the seven starters, had proved that they were serious cyclists. At the back of my mind I suppose that the spectre of the only other appearance of a British team in a big modern-day tour had been worrying me. In 1987, the ANC line-up had used their unique, mostly British image to brilliantly wangle a start in the Tour de France despite looking ill-equipped to take it on. By the end of the first stage of that Tour it was looking like a highly ill-judged enterprise, with team members struggling to keep pace with the rest of the field on what was essentially a straightforward, easy stage, straggling off the back into the slipstreams of following team cars and further into ignominy. It now looked likely that we could avoid that fate, anyway.

Things began well again in Terracina on the morning of the second stage. We were beginning to get used to the pattern of the start, everybody's favourite part of the day. After a hearty breakfast of cereal, fruit, bread rolls, croissants, eggs and sometimes pasta for those who wanted, we would unload into all the vehicles. Renault Laguna No.1 was driven by Sean, who would have one of the three mechanics in the back for the stage – Craig, our head mechanic, or Topper or Gianni, hired for the race. One of the three would be with Chris Lillywhite in Renault Laguna No.2, whilst the third would leave in the big Renault truck with Adrian Timmis straight after breakfast and drive directly to that night's hotel. The next vehicle in line would be the Renault Espace, which was the *soigneurs'* main vehicle for the stage, usually driven by Serge, an extremely genial French ex-copper from near Lille who was usually our first call when we needed an extra leg-rubber. For the journey to the start, the Espace was the riders' favourite, and pole position was invariably taken by Max, who would monopolise the front seat with his feet up on the generous dashboard.

We also had a mobile home with us, driven by some great Italian guys from a macrobiotic food company. They drove from hotel to hotel, cooking for us, as the vegetarian thing worked better at some places than others, and at least with them we knew that we would always be able to get a decent meal. They drove to the finish each day, usually with Raymond, another *soigneur*. Raymond was retired and living near Nice after running a VW dealership in Yorkshire for most of his life, but his first and last love was cycling. His was the face most welcomed by the riders when they streamed mud-caked and sweaty over the finish line after a long stage.

The riders who couldn't get in either of the team cars or the Espace got in my hired Ducato. This was to be avoided at all costs, because I would be carrying the invited sponsors, itinerant journalists and visiting guests, who were not the insular riders' chosen company. For most of the race I had Wilderness Man alongside me to help with the driving, organisation, car cleaning and general cattle-herding of our inmates.

Once the start was found – not always the straightforward task one might think – we would begin the morning's ritual stroll into the movable tented village that sprang up every day. Negotiating the scrum of fans, a quick flash of your pass at the neanderthal on the gate would see you through for some free coffee darker than night and thicker than mud. Then on to the free pizza, *non carne grazie*, and a free *EstaThe* (if you enjoy a soft drink that tastes like petrol), before hiding behind a free copy of the *Gazzetta* for ten glorious hassle-free minutes if you were Sean. The rest of us would catch up with people met the day before, talk in broken French or, even more daringly Italian, or just star-spot.

Matt and Ciaran were approached by a softly spoken Englishman at the start that morning, asking if he could have his photo taken with them. They were only too happy to oblige, and were a little surprised when he explained that he was Paul Smith, the fashion designer. 'Yes, I thought I recognised you,' managed Matt quite brilliantly. A massive cycling fan, Paul had broken off from some work in Milan to travel down and sample the Giro first hand, whilst lending some support to the McCartney boys. Matt was especially taken with him, and they remain in contact to this day . . . Matt still hasn't managed to prise a free suit out of him, mind.

The event of the morning was invariably Pantani's arrival. He would depart the Mercatone Uno mobile home separately from his teammates, accompanied by two burly minders. I am certain that protection was only these chumps' secondary role: there is no doubt that their main task was to inflate the legend and importance of *Il Pirata*, who alone or amongst his Mercatone brethren could have slipped around unnoticed by many. This theory was confirmed later in the year at the start of a race in Imola, when the stooges, jogging alongside the mounted baldie, steered him across a virtually deserted town square to find a couple of chaps innocently chatting to each other with no notion of the champ's impending arrival. They were unceremoniously shoved out of the way to let the great man past, despite being the only people within a 50-yard radius. Brilliant.

But the Giro crowd absolutely adored Pantani, and once whipped into a frenzy by his publicity-friendly approach, they would throng around him, yelling, '*Marco! Marco! Vai Marco!*', unsuccessfully thrusting pens and autograph books under his nose until he escaped through the gate into the sanctuary of the *Villagio*.

The Espace and the Ducato would leave about ten minutes before the off, dodging round on to the course and enjoying a fantastic drive on closed roads in front of waving fans all day. The Espace would drive to the feed zone, where Serge and Claude, the fourth masseur, would leisurely get the riders' food bags ready for collection in a couple of hours' time. When the bags were swinging gently over the stationary wing mirrors and the day's chats with the other teams' *soigneurs* were complete, the front seats would go back, two pairs of podgy feet would appear on the dashboard and the unmistakable sound of French snoring would drift out into the Italian spring until the race rolled up.

Wilderness Man and I would set out with our ever-changing cargo of guests to the first of several stops to cheer the boys on during the day's activities. With collections and drop-offs at various far-flung airports, transfers from start towns and finish towns to various hotels, and a total of 12 journalists, 28 sponsors, 16 potential sponsors, 15 riders' family members and 30 sponsors' guests in tow at one time or another, the Ducato racked up an average of 1,000 kilometres a day. Fortunately, the second Ducato held up rather better than the first, and saw us right through to the end.

That second stage wound down the west coast further and further south from Rome, reaching the outskirts of Napoli and a small town called Maddaloni. Here, the route passed through the finish line before sweeping round a mountainous 40 km loop and back down again. It was a 30-degree day, and the pace was just about manageable, with workhorses like Bjornar and Maurizio making frequent trips back to Sean's car for more drinks and sun cream for everyone, and the race reached its first pass of the finish line without too much hardship. Then, seemingly in an instant, everything changed. A thunderstorm broke, and the most torrential rain smothered the roads in a treacherous mixture of earth, water and oil, as the deposits of dirt, diesel and petrol left on the roads in a region dry for weeks immediately became a slippery mess. In addition, the temperature plummeted from a high of 30 to a shivery 12 degrees.

From the TV in the pressroom it was easy to see how difficult things must have been, as instead of riding in the usual close formation, riders were fanning out and leaving a few yards between them and the next man in either direction. Huge plumes of water rose off their wheels as they trudged over the poorly surfaced little mountain road that the organisers had picked out to make the finish of the day more interesting.

'Those must be the worst conditions I have ever seen in a bike race,' remembers David McKenzie now. 'There were huge rocks and masses of gravel just washing off the hillside and onto the road. It was so slippery that you just didn't want to be in touching distance of anybody else.'

Inevitably, people started falling off. 'I crashed quite early after it started; people were falling off all around. In fact, there was probably more guys hitting the tarmac than were staying upright!' laughs Dave.

If you had to bet on a McCartney rider falling, you'd put your house on Matt Stephens, or 'Lucky' as he would become known. Over the course of the season, he had an interface with the road surface worthy of note on eight or nine occasions. One of these came a couple of minutes after Macca's brush with the road.

'There was a group of us that all came down on a corner,' explained Matt, 'but I was OK and I jumped straight back on. I was chasing to get back up to what was left of the bunch when someone else went down right in front of me. It might have been Chepe Gonzalez, I'm not sure. On a normal day, I would have braked, steered round him and that would have been that, but as soon as I touched the brakes, the bike locked up completely.'

With the race beginning to break up considerably, Sean was further up the road, behind the main pack. Chris Lillywhite was just behind Matt when he hit the deck for that second time.

'He slid the bike sideways for about ten metres, no grip whatsoever. All of a sudden, he's hit a patch that's not as greasy and the bike's flicked straight and sent him flying, right on his knee,' said Cel. 'He didn't get up, and I thought that was it, especially when the ambulance showed up as me and Topper were jumping out of the car.'

Two Italian St John's-types, keyed-up and ready for action, leapt out of the ambulance and rushed up to Matt with their stretcher, delighted to be able to use those long hours of preparation at last.

'I was a bit dazed at first,' said Matt, 'but then I thought, "Hang on a sec here, I haven't spent all my life waiting to do a major stage race just to give up on the second stage," and I decided I wasn't quite ready to abandon.'

'Next thing I know I'm virtually wrestling with this ambulance bloke, trying to get Matt back off the stretcher and onto his bike,' said Cel.

'He's got one arm and he's going "No, no", I've got the other arm and I'm going "Yes, yes", and eventually we got our way and pushed Matt back off into the rain. The crowd were loving it.'

The fans at the side of the road were yelling 'Bravo, bravo', as Matt rode off dripping blood from a hole in his knee. One little old fellow in particular looked like he'd just seen the best entertainment of his life and hammed it up wildly for the cameras with some theatrical celebrations for the wounded Englishman.

By the finish, the day's carnage was clear for all to see, riders dripping home in ones and twos, shivering and sodden, desperately looking for their team helpers in the chaos of the congested finish area. The bus driver and doctor from Farm Frites with whom I'd been enjoying a sunny *gelato* only an hour previously were now waving and shouting manically to try and attract their riders' attention. Raymond, so calm normally, was on the verge of a heart attack, careering between the log-jammed vehicles carrying a bundle of towels for anybody dressed in yellow and blue that he could find.

The riders were eventually all in, warming slowly in the steamy confines of the motor home, Matt arriving at the very back of the field, now in last place overall but crucially still in the race. The knee was not looking good.

Stage Three was as beautiful as the back end of Stage Two was horrid. The route took in some of the most beautiful roads I have ever seen, hugging the cliffs and coastline that run south from Napoli with breathtaking views and sheer drops to the rocky shores punctuating the way. It was against this backdrop that Julian formulated one of his more imaginative ideas that would sadly never see the light of day:

'Next year, we'll hire a luxury gin-palace cruising boat and buzz along the coast for the first week, stopping off every now and again to watch them come whizzing by . . . the corporate entertainment types'll love all that.'

The day's racing went really well, with the finish in Scalea throwing up a nice surprise:

CIARAN POWER TAKES CAREER BEST RESULT

Ciaran Power of the Linda McCartney Pro Cycling Team landed the best result of his nascent professional career when he finished fifth on Stage Three of the Giro d'Italia today.

'Yes, I'm very pleased, but I know I can do better than that,' said the young man from Waterford, who turned 24 last week.

There was a great send-off from the start area for Matt Stephens this morning. The British rider's double crash yesterday had caught the imagination of the crowd and TV audience, who were delighted to see Matt leap off the ambulance stretcher and back on to his bike to finish the stage. Despite a great deal of stiffness in his left knee and calf, Matt was able to start today, and more pertinently, able to finish.

'It hurts when I get out of the saddle, and I feel as if I'm "square-pedalling" a bit,' said Matt afterwards. 'But there's 18 days to go in this race, and I reckon that's plenty of time to get better. Today should have seen me over the worst.'

The race today took in the beautiful and breathtaking Tirreno coast road from Paestum down to Scalea. There were many rises, falls and twists in the route, but when the *peloton* finally reached the finish loop of 25 km, there were still 50 or more riders remaining at the front, including Ciaran, Max Sciandri and Tayeb Braikia. Just as they were thinking about the finish for Tayeb, the Dane punctured, leaving Max and Ciaran to fight it out with the best sprinters.

'The whole field was in one long line, and it was really hard. I tried to speak to Max, but we both had our hands full just trying to hold a place in the line,' reported Ciaran as he enjoyed a massage in the hotel afterwards. 'As the last 3 km came up, I started to feel pretty good, and when Cipollini came past on the back of the Saeco train, I jumped on his wheel.'

Cipollini went all out for the line, with Ciaran and the others flat out alongside him. Jan Svorada, the Czech from Lampre flew up the outside of Cipo, who veered menacingly into his rival's path to cross the line first. The Lion King unsurprisingly found himself disqualified, and Svorada awarded the stage.

Almost unnoticed in the subsequent mêlée and media madness, Ciaran Power had clinched the best result of his career, and a great finish for Linda McCartney. Never having been in this position approaching the finish in a race such as the Tour of Italy, Ciaran felt he could have been more positive, and the experience has given him a big confidence boost.

'Next time I'm in this situation, I'll win,' he vowed.

John Deering
Linda McCartney Pro Cycling Team

Ronnie Power was actually quite hard on himself. We were calling him Ronnie now in acknowledgement of the proper Irish pronunciation of his name, stressing the second syllable, CiaRON. 'I let myself get muscled off Cipo's wheel a bit, which I wouldn't have done if I'd have been a bit more sure of myself. All good experience though, I suppose.' I thought that he would have been delighted to have got fifth, but he was disappointed to have got that close without going nearer to a win, which must be a good example of the excellent attitude Ciaran had since day one.

There was more good news for us the following day, when it was Tayeb's turn to mix it with the big boys and get in the top ten again, this time ninth in the sprint, behind that man Cipollini again. Smarting after his disqualification 24 hours previously, Cipo stormed to the line to register his 30th (yes, I did say *30th*) stage win in the Giro.

The morning had started with a good laugh too – Matt was profiled in the *Gazetta*, his death-defying crash recovery making good copy for the paper. He was billed as 'The Vegetarian in the Black Jersey' – a colloquialism describing the last rider in the race, usually known as the *lanterne rouge* in French- and English-speaking races. There was another glorious Stephens moment waiting in a hotel a little way up the road . . .

Lifting his heavy bag of neatly folded clothes into the lift, Matt thought he'd rest his knee by avoiding the stairs. Pressing the button for floor five, he leaned against the lift wall, rocking gently as the rickety elevator slowly groaned its way up the building, and waited. And waited. The lift had come to a standstill with the customary 'ding', but the doors failed to open. 'Hello?' enquired Matt, nervously. '*Pronto? Ciao?*' he experimented, but no response. Panicking now, he scrabbled wildly at the doors, fingers wedged into the gap, manfully attempting to pry them open. Should he try the alarm button? He was shouting by now, 'Heeelllp!' It was at about this moment that he heard a small noise from behind him, and he turned around. You know the type of lift where the doors on the other side open on some floors? Yep. It was one of them. When the lift had stopped at his floor, the doors behind him had glided back soundlessly. And on the landing looking in were three skinny Italian cyclists in tracksuits, silently relishing Matt's discomfort. Could that small noise have been a suppressed giggle?

The race wound on around southern Italy. Sean celebrated his 40th birthday with a huge floppy *EstaThe* top-hat bearing the legend 'I am 40!' thoughtfully supplied by the team, and was bought a five-litre can of his favourite olive oil to take home after moaning that Pippa had rationed his supply because he was costing them too much money. In the south of Italy the price of olive oil is closer to the price of water, rather than the price of champagne like it is in Sussex.

We stayed one night in a hotel that was in the middle of a jungle. I know you're not meant to get jungles in Europe, but I'm telling you this was a jungle, snakes on the road, all sorts. The reason I remember it is because the Arse were playing in the UEFA Cup final, and Cel and me were giving poor old Sean the Arsenal fan a really hard time. It went to extra time and I think penalties, but by then he'd slunk off to his room to watch their sorry defeat alone, as he had had his fill of us.

A little earlier, Wildie and me were beating a path through the vines in the Ducato when we suddenly came across a strange family of bewildered beasts, standing confused and caught motionless by our headlights, miles from anywhere. We inspected the animals, careful not to make any sudden movements or sounds that might disturb them until we were certain of their species. Yes, that's right, we had stumbled across the Banesto team staff. Hopelessly lost, and at the peril of the big cats probably lurking in the shadows, Ecchavari and his men greeted us like saviours, and piled into the back to be taken home. Interesting that he could lead Pedro Delgado and Miguel Indurain to six Tour de France victories between them, but couldn't lead a few mechanics on an evening stroll . . .

The next day was a Calvary for two of the best guys on the team.

CIARAN AND BJORNAR SURVIVE NIGHTMARE DAY

Ciaran Power and Bjornar Vestol overcame their own personal nightmares to get through the fifth stage of the Giro d'Italia. A stomach upset laid them both low, and for a while they stared elimination from the race in the face.

'When you're racing at this level, even if you're feeling 90 or 95 per cent, you're going to struggle,' said their manager Sean Yates, a veteran of 20 major tours in his days as a pro. 'When you feel like that, the aim has to be to finish, and set your sights on another day. If you're not protecting a high overall position, it doesn't really matter if you lose time, survival is all that counts.'

The tempo of the racing was slow for the first half of the race, but when the acceleration came, it was brutal.

'I was flat out in the gutter in the crosswinds, when I punctured,' said David McKenzie. 'I bumped along on a half-inflated tube for a couple of miles praying for it to ease up, and luckily for me they slowed up a bit just as I took a new wheel. Otherwise I'd probably still be out there!'

It was this acceleration that initially caused the problems for Ciaran and Bjornar. 'You know what it's like when you've been sick,' said Ciaran. 'You use up all your energy, and you feel like there's nothing in the tank. I had stomach cramps too by then, which didn't help.'

The pair struggled together over the mountainous roads that comprised the last 70 km of the stage, desperate to reach the pretty Adriatic coastal town of Peschichi inside the time limit. They had to finish within 10 per cent of the time set by Danilo Di Luca, the young Italian who had just taken the day with a blistering late attack further up the road. They scraped in, tired and relieved, last men out on the road.

Spirits were remarkably high at the hotel later. 'Yes, well, we made it!' grinned Bjornar as he rested in bed and refuelled his tired body with yet more peanut butter.

'We both feel right as rain now,' reported Ciaran. 'Nearly everybody will have one bad day in a three-week race like this. You're putting your body through so much, sometimes it complains a bit. But we've got through our bad day, and I think we'll be fine now.'

It was a good day for Matt Stephens, who tested his injured knee by climbing in the front group up the day's major climb late in the stage. There was also a great surprise when a bunch of local lads rigged up a huge 'Forza Stephens Matthew!' banner at the side of the road.

'I couldn't believe my eyes! They must have seen my crash and read about me in the *Gazzetta*. I wish I'd been able to stop and shake their hands, I've never seen anything like it!'

John Deering
Linda McCartney Pro Cycling Team

The race continued its progress, now heading north up from the boot of Italy along the warm Adriatic coast. Though it was well past Easter, it appeared the holiday season in Italy was still a long way off, and deserted towns and hotels welcomed the race with open arms. They were dog days for a press officer in love with cycling, and some of the most enjoyable times of my career with Linda McCartney. The team was performing well, Max in particular looking very strong, and the sense of team spirit tangible. There was time for swimming in the sea and working by the pool, and the opportunity to meet some really interesting visitors. One of the more amusing interludes involved the *Independent on Sunday*'s Andrew Longmore, who arrived at Bari airport the day after I expected him to . . . whoops. A day on the Adriatic coast was wasted. Nice coffee down there, decent paninis too . . . *Non carne*, of course.

I felt divided loyalties and some pangs of jealousy on the morning of Saturday, 20 May. Two of our number had headed back to England for the FA Cup final – Andrew to cover it for the *Independent on Sunday*, and Cel, gleefully clutching his Wembley ticket. 'Come on you blues!' I mustered as he left, a big part of me wanting to be travelling with him. We agreed that my commitment to the Chelsea cause would have to amount to no more than discarding my Asics T-shirt for the day in return for my Gus Poyet No. 8 jersey.

It was ironic then that my guest for the day was Dean Jackson of Asics, but he was more than understanding. In fact, he absolutely loved his day out, spending time in the bus and in the team car with Sean, getting a real feel for things as the race wound away from the coast into some beautiful countryside.

The first sign of excitement that morning came in a phone call from Sean. I was cruising along some deserted roads well in front of the race, when Sean rang, saying, 'Macca's attacked, and he's away on his own. Can you find out if he's got a chance of taking the Intergiro jersey?'

The Intergiro is a peculiar little competition where they draw a line across the road about halfway down each day's route, and the rider with the best record to this point wears a blue jersey. Yeah, brilliant idea, eh? So, I did a bit of homework and reckoned that Dave would move up to second or third in that, but would win a tidy little prize and get some recognition anyway. I phoned the boss back to tell him, and asked, 'Are you going up?'

'Nah, not worth it, I'll stay behind the bunch. I've sent Keith up.'

Keith Lambert had arrived that morning on a short-term lease to replace Cel. Now he was driving a team car in support of a lone leader in the Giro d'Italia.

So how does somebody plan a long break in a big race? Is it just on a whim, or do you study the race route for days? David McKenzie explains:

'I'd spoken to Sean a few days before, and said I fancied going for a long one. They don't often come off, but the longer you can stay out there the better – might as well get some good coverage for yourself and your team as sitting pretty in the bunch.'

'Macca had matured into a really good rider,' says Sean. 'We'd brought him in as a sprinter after he knocked out a couple of very fast finishes for the Australian squad at the 1998 Prutour, but he'd reinvented himself by the time we'd got to the Giro. He knew that he wasn't quick enough to beat the very fastest; the Cipos, the Zabels, the McEwens, so he looked hard at himself and considered how best to be a good pro.'

It was Robbie McEwen that Dave had been chatting to after the start that morning. About 18 km had passed by at a leisurely pace, and the two Aussies were rolling along with little effort at the heart of the bunch. 'I told Robbie that I'd been thinking about having a go at a long one. We were just coming to a little rise in the road, and Robbie, laughing, said "Go on then, mate, now's your chance!" Laughing back, I said "Right!" and just took off. The Italians were all up for a nice gentle Saturday morning and I got a bit of grief as I shot up the hill. They semi-chased for a few minutes, just a little way behind me, but the thought of being caught so quickly was so embarrassing I put my head down and kept going. After a little while I was free on my own, and I knew I must have a reasonable gap as they let Lego come up in the team car.'

There were still 164 km to cover that Saturday when Dave had said goodbye to Robbie McEwen; 100 miles. 'Sean told me that you think about all those miles of training you put in as a kid when your mates were out enjoying themselves, and how everyone was laughing at you and thinking you were wasting your time. The long break is when you think about payback, proving to everybody that it was worth it, making them sit up and notice.'

Keith was alongside Dave as often as the *commissaires* would allow, chatting, encouraging and cajoling, as was Gianni, the huge Italian mechanic in the back seat for that day.

'I thought about Susan, back in Toulouse and all the support she'd given me,' said Dave. 'I thought of my family, down in Melbourne. I thought of my brother, Stuart, and everything he'd tried to do as a cyclist, and how I wanted to make them all proud of me.'

The hours ticked by and the gap remained between Dave and his reluctant pursuers. With a hilly 40 km loop to be completed after the finishing town of Teramo was reached, they were very confident of catching the tiring Aussie and setting up the sprinters like Cipollini and Quaranta for the finish after a blisteringly fast last hour.

I first saw Dave that day in Teramo itself, as he came through the finish line to start that 40 km loop. Wilderness Man and I crouched at the side of the road, hollering our support. By now he was being chased by a guy from Polti who had slipped the bunch and was powering along, eating into Macca's lead. A couple of minutes later the bunch flew by, and there was no question now: they were chasing for real, flat out in a long line.

Cycling fans have seen it time and time again, a brave character ekes out a big lead early on when the big guns aren't too interested, only to see it crumble as he tires and they get all their teammates working to bring him back. Caught, sometimes within sight of the line, he drags himself in exhausted behind his captors, barely able to speak, accepting a few claps on the back of commiseration and admiration. Only Dave *wasn't* tiring. He was pushing on wonderfully, forcing a big gear round in his inimitable little-legged style, egged on continually by Lego, over the climbs punctuating the 40 km loop.

'I went through a pretty bad patch with about 30 km to go,' admitted Dave later. Back at the finish, Pete and I were glued to the TV screen in the *soigneurs'* area a few yards beyond the finish line. *Soigneurs* fit perfectly into the macho boy-man world of professional cycling. They give off an air of 'been there, done that, shagged her', that is, frankly, embarrassing for enlightened new men such as myself. I'd much rather be off tree-hugging or male-bonding than mixing with these types, but needs must at times. So, there they all were, spread nonchalantly over the plastic chairs, T-shirt arms pulled up to avoid annoying tan-lines, hair gel carefully applied until the 'I really don't care how my hair looks' look is just right, looking for all the world as if they really couldn't give a monkeys who won. Except that, on this particular day, they had two interlopers in their midst – a fat, pink-faced Englishman in a Chelsea shirt shaking uncontrollably and a 6ft 4in. Aryan blond biting his fingernails to the quick.

It looked to us as though Dave had been through his rough patch and his style was coming back. Sean was on the phone constantly to us, and we were giving each other updates – it looked like touch and go, as the flying bunch had swallowed up the chaser from Polti, and now only Macca stood between the sprinters' teams and glory. With 10 km to go, the TV infuriatingly paused for a commercial break, and we looked at each other with haunted eyes. Surely, he wouldn't get this close and get caught? Dave didn't deserve that, but we'd all seen it happen before. The action flicked back on live, with the information that he still had one minute on the closing bunch.

'COME ON, DAVE!' yelled Pete at the top of his voice, causing the old suntanned farts waiting to rub legs a few seconds of apoplexy at such an outpouring of emotion. The old boy from FDJ in front of us recovered from his near-heart attack enough to give us a withering look before returning to his snooze. But on the other side of the finishing line, it wasn't like that at all. The *tifosi* had found a new hero, *il vegetariano*, who had bravely taken the fight to their stars all day, and they badly wanted him to see it through. The shouting grew as the big weekend crowd craned their necks to see if it was going to be Macca first down the straight, or Saeco or Mobilvetta's foot soldiers, or worst of all, Macca being enveloped in the last few hundred metres.

The phone rang again. It was Sean: 'He's going to make it! He's going to do it!'

Then, there he was, cruising joyfully down the finishing straight waving to the crowds, a hundred miles alone. Unable to control myself, I raced past the security cordon as Dave crossed the line and met him about 50 yards beyond it, virtually knocking him off his Principia. I've never felt so intensely proud of anybody in my entire life as I did at that moment.

Macca even managed a few composed words in English and Italian for the surrounding journos, then Sean arrived and the tears began to flow. Everybody was hugging each other and crying, then somehow we made our way through the throng into the winner's enclosure, where we waited for Dave to perform the obligatory winner's dope test before walking up on to the podium. The huge magnum of champagne was prised open carefully, and it looked for a moment as if Macca would do the coolest of cool things and sip gently from the bottle . . . but then he lost his nerve and coated everyone in a 50-yard radius in a joyful Schumacher-esque display.

The day belonged to David McKenzie of the Linda McCartney Pro Cycling Team.

Chapter 8: Money

I woke to see David McKenzie smiling in colour from the front page of the *Gazzetta Dello Sport*. Inside there were pages about his bravery and grit, all under the headline 'McKenzie wins – on salad!'.

It was a superb coup for the Linda McCartney organisation and a fantastic advertisement not only for Linda's range of food, but for the whole vegetarian lifestyle. We all felt sure that McVities, Heinz, Tim Treharne and Paul McCartney himself would be delighted back in England, and that this was really the start of something truly special.

The English press was hardly less effusive; there were great pieces in all the broadsheets, including a magnificent full-page profile of the team by Andrew Longmore, recently returned to London. Macca's result in Teramo had forced the curly-topped journo to totally rewrite his feature in the pressroom at Wembley, where Chelsea were squeezing past a lacklustre Aston Villa to win the cup for the second time in three years.

Looking back in the *Gazzetta*, I was startled to discover a photo of Macca and I topping a small story about the *ragazzone ufficio stampa* of the Chelsea *azzurra*. It seemed my own out-of-control celebrations the afternoon before had attracted the attentions of the Italian press, and they loved the fact that a fan of Gianluca Vialli's Chelsea was waving the flag at the Giro while Roberto Di Matteo was scoring the winner at Wembley . . . so many tie-ins for those lucky Italian headline writers! I felt a little sheepish, but decided my Mum would be pleased, and it was all good publicity.

Apparently not. I was in line for a mighty bollocking.

'What the fuck do you think you're playing at?' screamed Julian down the phone from Toulouse. 'I've just had to explain to Tim that no, you don't work for Autoglass, you work for Linda McCartney, so you'd better remember who pays your fucking wages.'

Apparently my ungainly antics had been captured by Eurosport, who had delighted in showing me making a fool of myself at the finish, leaping around in my Chelsea shirt with the sponsors Autoglass plastered across the front of it. I was embarrassed into a humbling apology, and I must admit I felt extremely down in the dumps, especially when Julian suggested I was more interested in getting my own fat face on the screen than helping the team. I was gutted, and apologised to Macca too for spoiling his moment of glory and stealing his limelight.

Dave didn't seem too bothered – he was still on a massive high anyway, and to give Julian his due he replied to my written apology by saying, 'No problem, it's history now.' As more positive publicity about the scenes at the finish and appreciative emails began to roll in back at HQ, I think he softened his view a bit more. When you're not in the slightest bit interested in football, as neither Julian or Tim are, it's hard to appreciate the place it has in many people's lives: part of me thought he should be grateful that I hadn't demanded the day off to see the game!

We used the papers as a great way of starting conversation with the impossibly beautiful girls working for the radio station sponsoring the race. They happily translated, explaining that a *ragazzone* is a 'beeg, beeg boy', and that *il corpulento* is, well, a fat bloke. I preferred *ragazzone*.

Unbelievably, it nearly became a Linda McCartney double that day. Max had been targeting the Prato finish for some time, partly because it was so close to his own home, but also because it was the sort of difficult stage where he could really shine.

MAX SCIANDRI TAKES SECOND PLACE IN PRATO

Max Sciandri achieved the best result for a British cyclist for a long time, when he finished second on today's stage of the Giro d'Italia. The Linda McCartney Foods rider came agonisingly close to taking an incredible double win for the team, after David McKenzie's fantastic win in Teramo yesterday.

Max, who lives near Prato, had earmarked this day for his own, and was determined to do everything he could to win. On one of the hardest stages, with 257 km and a great deal of mountainous road to cover, he was at the business end of affairs all day. When the move he was in split on the day's final climb, he and Filippo Casagrande of Vini Caldirola took on an inspired chase, and made contact with the leaders with just 20 km of racing remaining.

The group of eight men plunged down the winding final descent, desperate to hold off their pursuers. The pace was of kamikaze proportions, and looked to have claimed the chances of Mapei's Axel Merckx when he missed a bend and disappeared into the crowd lining the route. With Max's fearsome finishing speed, a second amazing Linda McCartney victory looked to be a strong possibility. However, Merckx, son of the great Eddy Merckx, proved that Max is not the only man in the bunch who can recover seemingly lost causes, and fought his way back up to the leaders with just a couple of kilometres remaining.

Now Mapei, with Merckx and Paolo Lanfranchi, had two riders in the eight-man group, and they used their advantage to pull off the old 1–2. Merckx attacked along the right-hand gutter and Lanfranchi sat up, giving him a small but crucial gap. He hung on to take the stage by a mere six seconds, with Max winning the dash for second with power to spare.

The Linda McCartney man punched the bars in dismay, victory snatched away. The team will spend the evening trying to convince their star man that second place on a stage of the Giro, and a key stage at that, is a fantastic result, and one that the team could only have dreamed of a short time ago. But Max, born in Derby 32 years ago to an English mother and

Italian father, is the type of man who will settle for nothing less than victory. After two great attempts in the last three days, maybe it will be third time lucky for the British Olympic medallist.

John Deering
Linda McCartney Pro Cycling Team

Max had to deal with the press who once again described him as a 'choker', somebody who had the talent and ability to win, but not the nerve. They didn't realise one crucial element of his failure to win in Prato, though:

'I had no idea Merckx had got back on,' he explained. 'I knew he had fallen, and I thought it was just the seven of us there. I didn't want to show my hand too much, as I guessed I ought to be the quickest of those left, also the Vitalicio riders in there were going for the overall lead, so I knew I could trust them to keep the pace high. I was waiting for the sprint, and then I see this blond guy go shooting past out of the corner of my eye. If I chase, I lose. If I don't chase, I probably lose. That's what happened.'

An hour before the end of the stage, I'd been walking up the finishing straight with Russell Downing who was living near Prato racing for his Italian Under-23 team. As we chatted and pulled apart the stories around the race, we saw a cyclist come riding out of the distance towards us, perfectly turned out in Lampre kit, including Rudy Project helmet and shades and a Fondriest bike.

'Hey Fonzie,' I nudged Russell, 'look at this poser – thinks he's Maurizio Fondriest.'

It was Maurizio Fondriest.

For the big guys, the racing started in earnest the next day, when Francesco Casagrande took over the pink jersey at the mountain top finish in Abetone. We stayed in a village halfway down the mountain. It was beautiful, except the streets were so narrow we couldn't get the vehicles up there and had to park a kilometre or so below the hotel.

When the special narrow local minibus arrived in the morning to take
the riders down to the cars, Tayeb was (as usual) the last down from his
room, and the bus left without him. He ended up having to walk down
the hill like the rest of us – except Sean, who ran down for our
entertainment, waving his fists at the jeers from up above, laptop bag
flapping out behind him. When Tayeb caught up with the others, he
was not best pleased.

'He had a face like a smacked bum,' remembered Matt. 'I don't think it
would have been so bad if we hadn't all burst out laughing at him.' It wasn't
the first – or last – time that the Dane had a sense of humour failure, but
I think we all agreed later that Tayeb was not the misery he sometimes
appeared. He simply didn't mind too much if people liked him or not, and
he wasn't afraid to speak his mind. It is a sometimes excruciating English
habit to be constantly nice even when we don't feel like it – we have to
acknowledge that if people aren't always pleasant and polite to us, it may
just mean they are being a bit more true to their feelings.

That morning became difficult for Matt, as the race began by
climbing back over the same mountain-top it had finished upon the
previous evening. It ought to have been a gentle *piano* up the
mountain, but a few young locals eager to make names for themselves
set about the field instantly. To make matters worse, the race started
ten minutes earlier than the programme predicted. I was walking back
casually to my van in the company of Ian, the team's bank manager
over from England, and Simon Withers from *Cycling Plus*, when we
were forced off the road by the approaching *peloton*. Pressed into a
wall as lycra, aluminium, carbon fibre and shaved flesh passed within
a bushy sideburn of us, I noticed that some riders had been caught out
too, and were already chasing the bunch.

'We went flat out up the mountain and, with no time to get it
warmed up, the old knee was playing up instantly,' said Matt.

The Ducato, trapped behind the action, pottered up the mountain
and down the other side in the interminable line of following vehicles
until we were stopped by a maniacally waving Spanish mechanic. One
of the Kelme riders had crashed and been forced to abandon, and he

wondered if I could carry his bike to the finish? Normally this would have gone on the roof of his team car, but as the unfortunate chap had not created a space by taking his spare bike, would I please do the honours? Loading his Look carbon frame into the van, I saw that his front wheel had a massive dent in it, and wondered what had happened. Matt was able to fill me in later on.

'We went over the top a little way behind the main field, and it started to rain. It was pretty fast on the descent and so it was really cold, too. The Kelme guy had a cape in his back pocket and he decided to put it on, so out it came. Almost immediately, the sleeve of this cape dangled down and started to get tangled up in his back wheel, and he rode along wobbling and yelling as he tried to tug the thing out. He gave it one almighty pull, and then things started to happen in slow motion . . . the jacket was freed, and he grinned at his skill . . . the momentum of his tug saw the jacket arc forward over his shoulder . . . went straight into his front wheel instead and he somersaulted straight over the bars.'

We headed onwards, enjoying three nights including a time-trial stage and a rest day on the coast at Bibione near Venice. Cyclists will always tell you that the most exhausting, demoralising and downright weird thing about stage racing is having to move on from one place to another every single day. Three days in the same hotel is nothing short of luxury, and the team's togetherness was very clear over those few days as we ate, drank, shopped and generally chilled out together. The Dolomites loomed ahead. From here on in, it was survival.

The heights of both the Marmolada and Gavia passes would have to be crossed before the weekend was out, with a stage finish at Val Gardena's ski-resort. The Marmolada was the middle of three monstrous climbs on the Saturday, but it was the tiny, snaking road of the Gavia on Sunday that held the public's awe.

I crept up the Gavia in the Ducato, the road barely wide enough to be safe on a good day – now it was thronged with people on either side. On my right, the mountain dropped away to oblivion, and weekend cyclists wobbled up between me and the edge, a brush of a wing mirror away from certain death. I was shitting myself.

Behind, in team car 2, Topper was being interviewed by Graeme Fife. Graeme is a brilliant writer, author of *The Tour de France*, and he was here researching for his new book, *Inside The Peloton*. In another little gig he had cannily landed himself, Graeme was recording a section for Radio 4's *The Food Programme*, where the team's vegetarian lifestyle would be put under scrutiny. As a result, our man was laden with recording equipment, and he pushed a microphone under Topper's nose as they climbed up between the screaming hordes behind the race that day. His voice took on the intense, whispering edge of an excited racing commentator just before the off on Derby day . . .

'I'm here in the team car on the Gavia with Steve "Topper" Taylor of the Linda McCartney Cycling Team. Now, Steve, you've been on the Tour de France, you're now on the Giro d'Italia, you've worked at the world's biggest races, you know how it feels for these brave men to conquer these outrageous mountain roads. Tell us if you can, Steve, what a pass like the Gavia means.'

'Well, Graeme,' replied Topper, all cockney deadpan, 'it's a cunt of a climb.'

At the top of the Gavia it was snowing. Then, as the riders began to head down towards the finish, it turned to sleet, then freezing rain. A hideous, hideous day, but all seven survived, and Casagrande kept hold of his pink jersey.

Matt was in big trouble. The two big days in the mountains had created havoc for his injured knee, and now he had to deal with a bout of bronchitis not helped by the dreadful weather. The doctor said that if anything the injury was getting worse, and if he wanted to race again this year, he would have to seriously consider abandoning.

'It was so frustrating,' remembers Matt, 'because generally I felt within myself that I was climbing in the front group fairly comfortably apart from that bloody knee. Then, when the bronchitis kicked in, it was like breathing through a straw.'

With the Dolomites beaten, it made sense to leave before the Alps got too close. 'I could make it through the next couple of days OK, but I thought that I could seriously damage myself when we hit the mountains again later in the week,' he sighed. His bag was packed for the last time that Giro, and he returned to Andrea in Crewe. Losing my housemate three-quarters of the way through our adventure was a bitter pill to swallow, but it turned out to be the wise decision. In Chester, his specialist told him that using the knee whilst injured had already pulled the joint out of alignment, and severe mountain passes like the Agnello and Izoard could have finished his season.

We had the pleasure of entertaining an unusual guest for a couple of days as the race headed south to the shores of Lake Garda. Dr Michel Oxenberg was interested in investing in the team to promote his new range of male cosmetics, and a tie-in with the Linda McCartney name seemed perfect. I picked him up from the airport and took him to his hotel a short distance from ours – a country golf hotel, formerly a royal residence that would have made Buckingham Palace look like a council house. He was a very interesting little fellow, no more than 5ft 5in., always but always immaculately groomed and dressed, with a mysterious accent somewhere between Copenhagen and Boston, and invariably accompanied by his special friend and business partner Teddy. Julian saw him as a very serious potential investor and we were determined to give him an exciting visit.

The day's racing hadn't been all that interesting – there was a big mountain pass, the Aprica, but situated near the start after two really hard mountainous days, so the riders were happy to cruise over it and file down the long, lush valleys to Brescia. Julian was in team car 1 alongside Sean, but primed to vacate the passenger seat in double-quick time at a prearranged point to be replaced by the good doctor. A few minutes before this event, Bjornar slid back through the bunch and raised his hand to indicate to the chief *commissaire* that he needed assistance from the team car. The familiar crackle of '*Leenda McCartney a gruppo*', came over the race radio, and Sean pulled out of his place in the long line of following cars, racing up to meet Bjornar just behind the *peloton*.

'Drinks,' panted Bjornar, as Craig reached into the big eski, handing cold drinks forward to Sean in the driving seat.

'Coke, water or Extran?' asked Sean.

'Extran,' replied the Norwegian. Sean offered Bjornar a carton of the energy drink through his window as the cyclist rode on alongside the car. Just as Bjornar reached across to take the carton, Sean withdrew it back inside the car. 'What do we say, Bjornar?'

'Extran, please.'

'Good boy,' giggled the boss, handing it over.

'Sank you,' grinned Bjornar through gritted teeth, sounding ever more like Arnold Schwarzenegger. He went on to accept another five cartons and some drinks bottles to carry up to his teammates, filling all his jersey pockets, two bottle cages, and finally stuffing the rest down inside his jersey.

'Now Bjornar, before you go,' said Sean, 'we have an important guest joining my car in the next few minutes.'

'OK.'

'What does this mean?'

'It meence I heff to take zer race apart.'

'Correct.'

Bjornar dropped the Principia down a cog, stood on the pedals and resumed his place in the group. Sean skidded to a halt a couple of minutes later alongside where we stood, Julian leaping out as we bundled the immaculate doctor into his seat, and they were off again. We can picture, meanwhile, Bjornar doggedly finding his teammates in the bunch and handing out the afternoon's treats, probably knackered by now from all this activity. Oxenberg had been in the car no more than two minutes when the radio crackled back into life, 'Attack! Attack! Leenda McCartney!' and the Viking was off the front on his own. What a man. The attack was brought back not long after, but once again, the team had proved itself more than adept at playing the PR game.

At dinner that night, I caught sight of Bjornar staring down at his plate. The macrobiotic food we were cooked each night was nice enough, but when you're getting virtually exactly the same thing each night, or at best variations on a theme, it can get very dull. Apart from the lack of meat, which didn't bother anyone by now, these guys apparently had decided that all dairy products, eggs, potatoes and tomatoes would be bad for us. Doesn't leave much, does it? The big feller slowly rose from his seat and headed out the front door of the hotel. Half an hour later, I saw him sat on his own in a nearby pizzeria, tucking into a vegetarian pizza that covered the table. Good lad.

I'd been passing by with Anders Bystrup, the main bike designer at Principia, and Cel, back flushed with the success of Wembley and Teramo, hungry for beer. Anders is a great guy, unbelievably knowledgeable about bikes, and in no small portion one of the reasons why Principia make some of the world's finest frames. He also has that habit common among Danes of being extremely fastidious about getting his English right – he says that Danish people, for instance, often get terribly embarrassed when they hear anglicised Danes like Peter Schmeichel and Jan Molby talking English with regional accents, even though we find that endearing as a rule. So, keen to fit in, and enjoying the company of two Londoners, he pointed out the ubiquitous 'Irish' pub selling Guinness that he thought Cel would like . . .

'I am thinking,' he began slightly falteringly, 'that this is very, very up your alley.'

On the short stage to the outskirts of Milan, the McCartneys showed they were still fighting when Ciaran and Tayeb were sixth and seventh in the sprint. Ciaran's father and brother were coming from Waterford to see him in the Alps, and the Irishman was determined to cross them successfully.

I haven't seen the number of grand tours Sean has, but I bet even he hasn't encountered many more horrible climbs than the Colle dell'Agnello. When I pulled up with my cargo of Sigma Sport boys, Extran men and the Power family behind the pre-race cavalcade an hour before the race came up, we'd been scaling hairpins for miles and miles. I'd had to turn the air-con off to divert more power to the engine, which was, quite frankly, struggling. Finally we joined the back of the cavalcade as it lay stationary at the top of the pass, the inhabitants passing out freebies and gifts to the fans crowding the road side. We wandered along the line of ridiculous little cars with huge plastic sweets or washing machines on their roofs, chatting to the friends we'd made since Rome, knowing that there would be few more opportunities with Milan fast approaching. I was talking to Bernard, who had spent the whole race driving a giant Kinder Surprise around, when a flash of colour caught my eye high up in the snowy peaks above us. 'What's that, the top of the ski lift?' I naively asked. 'No!' laughed the confectionery transportation maestro, 'it's the top of the pass!' I felt sick when I realised that we hadn't even got halfway to the top. I knew that Ciaran was tired – he had struggled to make the time limit the day before, and I couldn't bear to think of him getting to within two days of finishing only to be eliminated. I put on a brave face for his dad, but I could tell he was thinking exactly the same.

We drove on across the amazing alien landscape of the Casse Desert to the top of the Izoard and walked down through the crowd, pleased to see a Union Jack up there and hear some supportive shouts. But the Linda McCartney team paled into insignificance when the pre-race announcer's car came up and told the masses that Pantani was in the break. Imagine your local on Saturday night, packed to the rafters, and the landlord coming over the PA to shout, 'Free beer for everyone tonight!' They went berserk.

Before too long they were there, Pantani first, then Simoni, Casagrande and Garzelli, riding at the pace most of us descend at. Max wasn't too far down, cruising along well within himself, looking every inch the strongest man in the race, cool enough to flash us all a little smile as we yelled at him. The rest of the boys were safely in a *grupetto* at about 20 minutes – but no Ciaran. That horrible feeling in the pit of my stomach came back, and we looked way, way back down the mountain, seeing little shapes still appearing out of the trees hundreds of feet below. 'Don't let that be him,' I thought, struggling to pick out the colour of their jerseys. Then suddenly, from along the human tunnel of fans, we heard the by now familiar 'Hey Leenda!' shout, and there he was! Jersey ripped open to the waist, a look on his face that would make his mother cry, there was Ronnie Power, only a few seconds behind the *grupetto*. What a moment. We roared him on over the summit and he flew down the descent to Briancon, now safely back in the arms of the bunch.

I saw life at the sharp end of pro cycling a day later in the mountain village of Sestriere. Casagrande had carried the lead of the race ever since Abetone, nearly two weeks before. Now, with the end tantalisingly close, he lost his grip on the race when Pantani's bone-thin lieutenant Stefano Garzelli snatched it from him in the mountain time trial. As Casagrande was led past me at the finish, still on his bike but surrounded in a scrum of hungry journos, I could see the tears flowing down his pain-etched face as the enormity of his loss sunk in. He had lost nearly two minutes to Garzelli in an hour after spending three weeks building up a lead of thirty seconds.

Julian and Sean enjoyed the day massively. The team car's position in the pecking order is determined by where your best rider lies overall, and Sean had been forced to drive behind Teun Van Vliet's Farm Frites car for many days as the Dutch team car belched out horrific amounts of black smoke. Max caught their man on the climb up to Sestriere, and in doing so leapfrogged over him in the overall rankings. Julian, back out with us after moving house in Toulouse, leaned out of the passenger window and flipped Teun the finger as Sean cruised past behind Max. At the finish Sean grabbed the exuberant Dutchman in a friendly headlock and shouted, 'Now I don't have to breathe in your shit any more!'

'English bastards!' shouted back Teun, until they both broke down in fits of laughter . . . meanwhile Julian was peeling the number 18 off the Renault's rear window and carefully placing it over the old 17 on the Farm Frites car. 'Ha ha!'

Another great plan was materialising in Julian's mind . . .

'Next year, we'll hire a helicopter and buzz around the mountains for the last week, stopping off every now and again to watch them come whizzing by . . . the corporate entertainment types'll love all that.'

It sounded strangely familiar, and even less likely.

Some of us went to an extraordinary party on the banks of the river in Turin that night, a glittering and romantic setting to remind you of all the great things Italy has to offer. Most of our riders were far too tired to do anything but stay and sleep at the hotel, but myself, Sean, Craig, Topper and a few others ventured forth to drink a good deal of beer for the first time in three weeks. *Belissimo*. There was more cause for celebration the following night, when the whole clan gathered at our Holiday Inn in Milan to toast a resounding success. We had won a stage, contributed to the racing from start to finish, drawn plaudits from all quarters and generally justified our inclusion despite the most disastrous of starts. Fond farewells already exchanged with the new friends we had made, that last Sunday night was just for us as family joined us from all over for a long, long meal that lasted deep into the hot Milanese night. The Power clan helped me throw Sean fully clothed into the pool, though needless to say when I tried to help him out I ended up in there too, dragged in by one of those massive shovel hands. If you try this at home, I recommend making sure there's enough of you to grab a limb each, as they tend to kick and scream like a spoilt baby.

Back in Toulouse, work went on frantically. Julian spent longer than ever on the phone to all the sponsors, making sure they knew what we'd achieved. I put together a big file of press cuttings to push home the message. Tim Treharne had joined us for that last stage in Milan, and Julian was confident that he had secured concrete support for 2001 and beyond for the team – his big aim now was to use the McCartney name to bring in some big subsidiary sponsors who would essentially pay for the team's expansion. Paul McCartney had sent the team a congratulatory email via his secretary, saying, 'Linda would have been proud of you.'

Julian's biggest concern was the total apathy and lack of interest apparently shown by Heinz, the new manufacturers of Linda

McCartney food. Nobody there appeared to be aware of the things we were doing, despite our constant attempts to push news stories, videos of our achievements and ideas for marketing opportunities under their noses. One of our more bizarre attempts to curry favour and create interest was to take out a full-page advert for Linda McCartney Foods in *procycling*, showing Macca crossing the finish line over the legend – 'Linda McCartney Foods – the sweet taste of success', and paying for the ad ourselves! The PR and marketing company they employed made a point of ignoring us, not even bothering to reply to our invitations to join us at the Giro, never returning our calls and making no attempt to utilise what was now becoming a very strong marketing tool. One guy, the principal chef at Linda McCartney, Norman Brockwell, was tearing his hair out at his employers' attitude, going so far as to set up his own in-house newsletter to extol the team's feats. He would ride his bike to work at the factory in Norfolk in his Linda McCartney kit, only to be given quizzical looks by all and sundry there.

'It's unbelievable!' he complained, 'Even the people who work here don't know we've got a team!'

In the face of such laissez-faire behaviour, we decided to set up an event at the factory around the time of the National Championships a few weeks later. We were helped by a fellow who came to be our main champion at Heinz, Ian Jones, who came down to Norfolk from his office in Hull and set up a tour of the factory and some photo opportunities with the bosses.

What a hilarious day out. We got kitted out in full protective plastic hats, raincoats and boots for our tour of the factory, much to everyone's amusement. Pascal turned on his charm with every single woman working on the production line, despite his lack of any English to speak of. Needless to say, they loved it, but then anything must be better than stuffing broccoli into pastry for seven hours at a time.

Cel, who had pulled his plastic hairnet into a sort of Dickie Bird Yorkshire flat cap shape, started feeling a bit unwell.

'It was all those smells,' he explained, 'all that yucky, cheesy sauce being made, it just got to me.' Next thing we know, he's belting past us, vaulting a low wall into a washing-up area and vomiting noisily down a sink. Honestly, you can't take some people anywhere – especially if they've knocked the back out of six pints of Guinness the night before.

The best part of the day was a tour of Norman's kitchen, where all the new and exciting stuff gets made. It was like a set for Delia's kitchen – all real kitchen units and cookers but on a grand scale, with a huge table laid out with meat-free goodies. We tucked in; Pascal in particular looked like he hadn't seen a good meal in ages and did his best to clear the table single-handedly. Norman was resplendent in a white chef's coat, checked trousers and huge hat. He may even have been wearing a chequered neckerchief, but that may be my memory embellishing his outfit – I'm sure he didn't have a rubber chicken hanging from his belt, anyway.

Shortly afterwards, a package turned up addressed to me at the *service course* in Cornebarrieu . . . my very own Linda McCartney chef's smock.

That summer was to be a strange one. To the outside world, things were going from strength to strength . . . inside the camp, the story was a little different.

In July and August, wages started to arrive late, or not at all. It appeared that people like Matt, Ciaran and myself, who were not on super-high salaries, were getting paid OK, whilst guys a bit further away and earning big money, like Max, were being flicked. In August I drove out to Padova to meet the team for a few races around north-eastern Italy to find morale at an all-time low. I was shocked, as I had no idea that things were so bad, and I felt pretty embarrassed at not being in touch with what was going on.

'Come on John, you must know what's going on,' pleaded Max, but I didn't. Back at the *service course*, I didn't have a lot of contact with the others. I was happy to get on with my own work and got on well with the team and staff, so the business stuff didn't really concern me.

I'll try to piece together what was going on at that time with the benefit of hindsight and other people's thoughts . . . it has to be said that this is not a complete picture, nor will the complete picture probably ever be known. The best place to start the shenanigans is probably with the entry into our tale of an Australian working-class hero . . .

A major part of our plans for 2001 fell into place when we signed Neil Stephens to become co-director with Sean. Neil was one of the most highly regarded figures in the *peloton*, a gritty Australian who had been an integral cog in the yellow Once machine through the '90s, before becoming a very popular Tour de France stage winner with Festina. His image as a hard-working, honest professional was very similar to Sean's, but with one crucial difference: Stevo had been a rider in the Festina team thrown out of the 1998 Tour de France for doping.

Those readers who know all about the Festina affair can skip the next bit, but this is the main gist of it. On his way to the start of the 1998 Tour de France in Ireland (don't ask), Willy Voet, a *soigneur* for the French Festina team, is stopped by police on a back road crossing the border from Belgium into France near Lille. His car is full to the brim with performance-enhancing drugs, largely the infamous (and at that time undetectable) EPO. The team is thrown out of the Tour in disgrace, the race is brought to its knees by the ensuing police raids and scandal; arrests and court cases follow. The affair shook the sport to its very core, and for a while it seemed that the Tour de France itself could collapse. Fortunately for all of us that love cycling, the damage was partially patched by Pantani's character-fuelled win in that Tour, then Lance Armstrong breathing fresh human life into the race the next summer.

Two years had passed since that tortured tour when we announced that Stevo was to be our new co-director. We were delighted to have signed such a big name, moreover such a popular figure in English-speaking circles particularly. Mind-numbingly stupidly, with the benefit of hindsight, not Julian, Sean or myself had once considered the negative publicity that bringing in Stevo might create. All I can think now is that from the cosseted, busy world we were in, the 1998 Tour seemed a very distant memory.

The first inkling that we may have made a rod for our own backs came on the Tour de France in July, a few days after we had announced Neil's impending arrival. Most of the boys were enjoying a spot of downtime with their families after a hectic and overworked spring, while I was on a working holiday, networking and press-releasing from the Tour de France. I stopped for a chat one morning with Paul Sherwen, the Englishman who had been a long-time compadré of Sean's as a fellow pro, then latterly in the backroom at Motorola. For a fair few years, Paul had been co-hosting Channel 4's Tour coverage and was as a result a well-known face never short of an interesting point of view, so I took the opportunity to ask him what he thought of Neil's appointment.

'Surprised,' he said. I must have raised an eyebrow. 'Don't get me wrong,' he went on, 'I think he'll make a fantastic manager, but the PR implications of putting somebody so tainted by the Festina thing into the "Clean Machine" don't bear thinking about.'

Ouch. I couldn't believe we hadn't even thought about that. When I spoke to him on the phone that night, Julian agreed that it was amazing we hadn't considered it, but we hoped his popularity would shine through with the vast majority of people.

I'd had first-hand experience of that popularity a couple of days previously. I was seeing an English girl in Toulouse, and she was keen on a day out at the Tour. The Pyreneen stage to Hautacam was no great distance from Aussonne, so Liz and I drove down in the Espace. A bit of bullshit to the gendarmes at the bottom of the climb was enough to get us on to the race route, and we drove up the mountain an hour or two in front of Lance Armstrong – I had my foot down, but I wouldn't be surprised if he was quicker up there than us, such was his phenomenal performance that day. Stevo met us at the top with a couple of day passes. He was working out his notice with Oakley; the sunglasses manufacturer employed him to look after their sponsored riders at the races. As we chatted on the misty mountain, Neil accompanied by his Basque father-in-law, a four-wheel drive Mercedes slowed down to pass us and a familiar face looked out as the driver's window was lowered.

'Hey, Stevo, *que pasa*?' said Miguel Indurain. He stopped for a chat. Like us, he was there for the day out, with wife and kids in tow. Stevo talked to Mrs Mig, whilst the big man filled me in on the merits of his new car (good on the motorway, not so great off-road) and Liz played peek-a-boo with his two boys as you would expect from a good primary school teacher.

As they drove off to garner a good viewing spot, Liz asked, 'Who's that?'

'Just an old friend,' I replied nonchalantly. Or perhaps I said, 'Who's that? *Who's that*??? Only one of the greatest athletes of the twentieth century! Only the bloke who won this race five times! Back to back! Miguel bloody Indubloodyrain, that's who!' It was a long time ago, I can't remember.

In fact, over the course of that day, a lot of people stopped to say hello to the mulleted Aussie, especially Spanish people, who treated him like a superstar, his many years at Once making him a true man of the Basque Country in their eyes. He greeted all and sundry as an old friend, in English, Spanish, Basque, Italian, French and back to English, leaving me struck by how much people really *liked* this man. I liked him too, he was great. He told us how he had met his wife Amaia when she was working in a San Sebastian supermarket. He would talk to her every day, finding less and less convincing reasons to go shopping. One day, after queuing for ten minutes with one tomato despite all the other checkouts being free, he asked her if she'd like to meet him at a coffee shop after a bike race that was on in town that weekend. In his bumbling Basque of that time, he'd already told her that he was a cyclist, but she thought he meant he rode a bike to work or something; anyhow, they made the date. The 'local bike race' was actually the prologue of the Tour de France, making one of its biannual visits outside of the borders. When Neil arrived at the coffee shop, he apologised for being a few minutes late, having just finished his time trial, leaned £5,000 worth of low-profile up against the table, wiped down his pink skinsuit and sat down, unstrapping his aero helmet. When Amaia had finally managed to bring her lower jaw up to meet the rest of her mouth and Neil had signed the 63rd autograph for the mob now surrounding them, she said, 'So *that's* what you meant by "cyclist".' The rest is history.

The mixed messages surrounding Neil's appointment started to grow over the next month or so. One email I received from a fan said:

> As the team is supposed to portray healthy and clean living the appointment of Neil Stephens is a BAD move. It raises the never-answered question – not mentioned on your press release or in his CV – of his part in the face of overwhelming evidence in the 1998 Festina scandal.

On the same day, I received another saying, 'Great news, what a fantastic combination, Neil Stephens and Sean Yates!'

Things started to get a bit warmer when Julian had a call from William Fotheringham, cycling correspondent at the *Guardian*. Did we know that there was a new book out in France all about the Festina affair, and how Neil clearly admitted his guilt at taking banned substances? *Le Procès du Tour* by Fabrice l'Homme apparently explicitly detailed Neil's confession to police about taking both EPO and Human Growth Hormone.

Julian, sensing that Fotheringham was keen to go to town on such a lurid story concerning the self-proclaimed 'Clean Machine', put the phone down and thought for a moment.

'Right, that's it,' he said. 'We'll have to sack him.'

I counselled restraint. 'Hang on a minute. He hasn't even started properly yet.'

'Even more reason to nip it in the bud.'

'Let's project a few of the consequences and think about it first.'

It appeared to me that washing our hands of Stevo could cause more problems than it would solve. For instance, it was clear that his mere presence had brought a massive boost to our credibility and pulling power within the sport. At the Tour de France in July, riders like David Millar, Jens Voigt, Magnus Backstedt and Frank Hoj had all expressed their interest in the team and its long-term ambitions now that we had such a professional set-up. All the Spanish riders we were talking to were interested in coming because of Stevo. Both the clothing companies we had in line to supply the team in 2002 – Etxe-Ondo for racing gear and Oakley for casual – had been brought in by Stevo. The general buzz he had created within the team and in the wider surrounds of the sport as a whole felt like a big snowball rolling . . . I worried that losing him now because of a negative story that might never happen would be shooting ourselves in the foot.

Julian slept on it. He didn't want to lose Stevo any more than I did; he could see for himself the energy Stevo had already brought to the job and the impact he was having on our profile within the sport. The next day, Julian had a long and open chat with him about the various consequences. Stevo immediately offered his own resignation, but suggested a couple of avenues that might help. Most pertinently, Australia's cycling authorities had carried out an exhaustive investigation into Neil's role in the Festina affair before selecting him for the Commonwealth Games in 1998, and subsequently appointing him as a European liaison officer for Australian national squad riders.

Also, Neil was adamant that he had made no such confessions to the police. He had agreed that he had taken medicines and preparations given to him by team doctors under instruction, but denied vehemently that he had any idea they were EPO, Human Growth Hormone or any other illegal substance. For the police or M. l'Homme to suggest that he had directly confessed to using those products was at best a mistranslation and at worst a vicious slur in Neil's eyes.

I prepared two press releases, one detailing Neil's resignation, the other giving him the team's full backing.

Ray Godkin was one of the most respected men in Australian sports administration, and had been a trusty servant to the country during his tenure as president of Cycling Australia, the national governing body. At Julian's request, he sent a copy of the comprehensive dossier he had completed after his thorough investigation into Stevo's part in the Festina affair. There were contributions from people like the Australian Olympic Committee (AOC) Secretary General Craig McLatchey saying there was no impediment to Stephens ever representing Australia, plus legal advice from Brown and Co to the AOC and Australian Commonwealth Games Association that there was no evidence to warrant any action being taken against him. Its conclusion was emphatic: Neil Stephens had no case to answer.

'We have used him and are happy about doing so. He was endorsed with my blessing. He is a victim of circumstances beyond his control,' Ray Godkin told *The Australian*'s Rupert Guinness.

Julian made the decision we all hoped he would – Neil was to be kept on, supported and exonerated. His resignation had been refused. I pre-empted the bad press we were worried might appear by sending out our prepared statement giving Stevo the full backing of the team in the face of 'recent criticism and allegations'. I was extra-careful not to send the wrong one!

So, did Neil Stephens take drugs when he was at Festina? Quite frankly, I neither knew nor cared. From my point of view, he was a driving force for the team and a big plus in pushing us on into the really big league. In 1998, from what I can make out, substance abuse was pretty much institutionalised in much of cycling – turn up at the start of the season, here's your bike, here's your kit, here's your drugs. That certainly was not the case by 2000. While cheating still went on – and, no doubt, still goes on – it was largely each individual's choice and the onus fell on him to arrange it and carry the can. Of course, many teams turned a blind eye, and all would dread the positive test, but the feeling within the sport was that regimented, blanket drug-taking was a thing of the past. Of course, with an infallible EPO test still some way off at that stage, the temptation to boost performance was a great one, especially if you are riding under the belief that all your competitors are 'charging'.

Let me try to explain some of the attitudes towards drugs inside cycling. Firstly, the rule at that time was that no rider could have a haematocrit level of more than 50 per cent. This indicated the amount of oxygen carried by your red blood cells, and it was thought that a level of more than 50 per cent was generally a sign of EPO usage. The UCI decreed that a level of more than 50 per cent was dangerous, and a rider would therefore be excluded from a race on health grounds.

This rule was one of the strangest and least successful of all cycling regulations. Without an actual test for this potentially deadly drug, the UCI were tacitly allowing its use – as long as you didn't overdo it. Don't get headaches, don't do so much that you die of a heart attack in the middle of the night and embarrass us all, just cheat quietly, please. It made no allowance for the way that haematocrit naturally varies over the population, so some riders with a natural level of 48 per cent or 49 per cent would be racing against cyclists who would have naturally been at 35 per cent, but had carte blanche to artificially jack themselves up to the limit daily. Then there were the men who lived at high altitude, thereby obtaining a naturally high haematocrit. They could prove their innocence by providing doctors' certificates – suddenly, cyclists who could afford it were buying holiday homes high in the mountains and making out that they were living there ten months of the year.

Some people believe that this rule was the reason for a strange phenomenon in cycling in the late '90s and beyond – the finales of classic one-day races were being fought out by bunches of 40 or more, whereas a lone winner or the cleverest of a hardy group of three or four had traditionally been there at the end of such attritional affairs. Had the playing field been levelled so much by the 50 per cent rule that everybody was now the same?

There was also the strange concept of honour amongst thieves. Among many cyclists, it was acceptable to take the medications that other people were, yet other things were beyond the pale. There were often dark rumours about riders who would take anything to try and give themselves a boost. They were cheats, 'chargers'. This explains the strange fear and loathing of Armstrong in some quarters, i.e., 'He can't be that good, he's obviously got some wonder drug that the rest of us haven't heard of. Cheat.' How about getting so sick with cancer that your body totally changes shape, and you lose more weight than you ever imagined possible? Wouldn't that help you ride uphill? Do you think that riding a bike will hurt as much after you've undergone the pain of chemotherapy? No, it's clearly much easier to believe in a wonderpill.

And of course, there was the issue of professionalism. One of our riders had ridden as a junior for an Italian team. On the last day of a stage race, he worked his way into the winning move. The best-placed rider overall, he would win the race if he stayed with the break to the finish. On the last climb, however, he was dropped, exhausted. As he weaved across the road waiting for the bunch to inexorably swallow him up, his team manager drove up alongside. 'I've just realised,' said the manager, 'you're not taking any medication, are you? That's hardly a professional approach, is it? You've let your whole team down now by your selfishness and stupidity.' If this story doesn't give an insight into the pressures faced by young cyclists, I don't know what does.

How to stop bastards like this? God only knows – when winning is so important to people, somebody will always push the envelope. Surely the only way to beat them is to make sure that cheats get caught?

Chapter 9: Things We Said Today

Kevin Livingston had been one of Lance Armstrong's most loyal and trusted lieutenants throughout the golden boy's resurrection. His climbing talents and reliability made him a potential genuine Tour contender and he wanted to show that he was capable of more than helping somebody else win big races – he wanted to do it himself. That meant leaving the comfortable and rewarding surroundings of the US Postal Service team, where his future would be inextricably bound to helping Lance.

As an American, Kevin was a very attractive proposition to us. Not only did his new world English-speaking image fit in with the team's profile, Linda McCartney Foods were planning to launch their products in the USA.

So we signed him, after Kev agreed a contract of, I believe, £350,000 a year for two years with an option on a third, with various bonuses and incentives. Sean knew him from the days when Kev had been a raw youngster at Motorola and had always liked him; he went to stay with the American for a few days at his place near Nice and make plans for 2001. There was a little clan of US Postal guys down there; Lance liked to have Kev and Tyler Hamilton near him in a little ex-pat training community. Coincidentally, Lance himself had chosen Nice for his base because it had been Sean's home when the young gun turned pro and rode under Sean's wing at Motorola in the '90s.

'I saw Kevin as very much the pivotal part of the team in 2001,' said Sean. 'We were looking to build a more focused squad. Getting our name everywhere wasn't as important as it had been, and we wanted to concentrate on building a team that could really compete in stage races. Kev was the ideal team leader.'

I met Kevin at Paris–Brussels late in the summer. He was excited about coming to us, and wonderfully helpful and articulate.

'I need to find out how good I'm going to be,' he told me. 'I had offers from a few teams, but all of them wanted me to go and help their leaders, still a *domestique*. A well-paid *domestique*, but a *domestique*. What's the point? I already work for the best team leader in the world, and he's my friend.'

KEVIN LIVINGSTON JOINS LINDA McCARTNEY

The Linda McCartney Pro Cycling Team have signed US star Kevin Livingston to lead the squad in 2001. The 27-year-old climber is leaving US Postal Service after two years' dedication to Lance Armstrong's Tour de France assaults. It is no coincidence that his two seasons at USPS have seen Lance stand on the top step of the Paris podium twice in succession.

'The time was right for me to spread my wings a little,' says Kevin of his decision to sign with the British squad. 'At US Postal, my whole programme was geared to peaking for the Tour de France, so I would be in the best position to help Lance. But it also meant that I rarely had a chance to ride for myself and win races for Postal in my own right. At 27, I ought to be approaching my best years, and I need to find out how far I can go.'

With four Tours de France under his belt, including a fine 17th overall for Cofidis in 1998 and two wins for his team leader in the subsequent years, Kevin's CV is impeccable. 2001 is the year he has earmarked for some personal victories, and for Linda McCartney glory. 'I'll be sitting down with Sean Yates and Neil Stephens over the coming weeks to work out a programme of racing, then I'll know what my big targets will be,' explained Kevin.

John Deering
Linda McCartney Pro Cycling Team

Kev was extremely helpful on the press side of things. Coming from a country like the USA where cycling has been a minority sport in a similar way to the UK, he knew the importance of good press. He put me in touch with lots of journalists back home eager to follow his progress. He was very friendly, very keen and a pleasure to know.

When Lance found out, he was livid. He demanded absolute loyalty from his friends and teammates: this was treason. Sean became persona non grata *chez* Lance from that day forth.

Not long after Kevin signed his contract, we began to sense a sea change. His management, involving both his father and well-known American riders' representative Bob Mionske must have got wind that all was not well at Linda McCartney. After much negotiation with Julian and Tim Treharne, they asked that his wages be paid in advance for 2001, a condition that was impossible for us to meet. Later events would show just how unfeasible it was.

Clearly pretty astute types, the Livingston camp had kept a couple of irons in the fire. Lance's displeasure with his former friend meant there was no return to US Postal, but the next best thing was very much an option – riding for Lance's arch-rival, Jan Ullrich at Telekom.

In November, we conceded defeat – there was no way Kevin Livingston was ever going to ride for Linda McCartney. Instead, he would go on to become a tower of strength in Ullrich's attempts to unseat Armstrong from his Tour de France throne.

The press release was an embarrassing U-turn . . .

KEVIN LIVINGSTON

Here is an update on the situation regarding Kevin Livingston and the Linda McCartney Pro Cycling Team.

In September, Kevin signed a pre-contract agreement to join the team, but as of now his contract is still to be finalised.

'I spoke to Kevin again last night, and there are still some important details to be ironed out before Kevin becomes a Linda McCartney rider,' explained general manager Julian Clark. 'Negotiations continue. The contract is on the table.'

'Of course, we want Kevin to come, but I think we will be a very strong outfit with or without him,' added team manager Sean Yates. 'He may decide to go to a team that can offer him a guaranteed start in the Tour de France – something that we're not yet able to do. The positive side of the situation is that we are in negotiation with a couple of other riders, so we will not be at a disadvantage whatever happens.'

Kevin has promised to make a final decision about 2001 before the end of the month.

John Deering
Linda McCartney Pro Cycling Team

Within days, *cyclingnews.com* was reporting:

Kevin Livingston has joined the Deutsche Telekom squad. The 27-year-old resident of Austin, Texas made the announcement on Monday from the team's training camp in Dresden, confirming an earlier rumour that he would join the Telekom Train. 'I had actually signed a preliminary agreement with the Linda McCartney team, but when there were financial problems, I made contact with Telekom boss Walter Godefroot,' said Livingston. 'I am looking forward to my new role. The Telekom team ranks among the best teams in the world.'

Our salary cheques for July bounced, but those of us in Toulouse got paid again quickly. We were all banking with the local Credit Agricole, who were incredibly supportive and understanding. They probably could have afforded to add another big name to their squad if it hadn't been for us.

As I mentioned earlier, I drove out to Padova to be met with some serious discontent. Short of handing out cash, there wasn't too much I could do to buck up spirits, but they were a very professional bunch by now, and recognised that racing well would be the best way out of a sticky spot for everyone. Sean did a fantastic job of getting everybody up and ready for action for a series of big races, the first of which was the Giro del Veneto.

We were staying in the strangest of places. Just outside of Padova are a series of little spa towns very popular with visiting Germans and Austrians. The warm sulphuric springs that rise in that area are siphoned by big old-fashioned hotels into swimming-pools and the like for Germanic wrinklies seeking the secret of eternal youth. I'm no Mephistopheles, but I'll be damned if they'll find it in those infernal places. We were shouted at for going in the pool without a swimming hat on – fair call as it turned out, as most of the other guests were there searching for a cure for leprosy. Or something like that. Creeping down for a silent swim after dinner was a good way of avoiding the old gits, as they were all sleeping off the soup they'd sucked through a straw by then. I thought I'd try the same trick for an early-morning dip, but was surprised to find the corridors a hive of senile activity at half-past-stupid.

As I brushed past walking corpses in varying states of decay, I noticed a lot of them were gravitating around a room off to my left. I slowed as I passed the doorway, sneaking a view like a camera panning slowly round a doorframe. Inside was a scene like something from an Iain Banks novel, or a futuristic nightmare like *Brazil*. Rows of old people sat facing the wall in little individual booths. The booths were reminiscent of telephone cubicles, like those you might find in an old-fashioned press-room, or listening booths in '60s record shops. Except there were no phones: instead, a snaking thick plastic tube sprouted from each booth, attaching itself to a mask strapped to the well-used face of each grateful old prune that sucked in the supposed healing gases straight from the bowels of the earth.

Dropping my towel in shock, I swallowed a scream and ran back to my room to hide under the bedclothes, promising myself that it was just a bad dream and I would wake up soon.

The inmates of Room 229 were Benny Van Brooks, as we were now calling the Australian-would-be-Flandrian, and Lucky Stephens. It would be a day to remember for both of them. The Giro del Veneto starts in the piazza in the centre of Padova. It's an extremely popular event, as Veneto is the bike-manufacturing centre of Italy, and as Italy is the bike-manufacturing centre of the world, you've got yourself some *real* fans here. Italy is the place to be for bike racing in August, anyway: things always hot up in the scramble for places for the Italian World Championship team, the *squadra*, with even more pressure on the selectors in Olympic year. The racing is of unbelievably high quality, with races that you or I have probably never heard of drawing huge crowds and fields to match that of any World Cup race. Men like Francesco Casagrande, Michele Bartoli and Davide Rebellin are the masters here, riders who can come up with the goods time and time again, week in, week out. One of their number, Stefano Zanini of Mapei, rides past me over the cobbles of the piazza, one hand resting lightly on the bars as he chats to his small son . . . who is seated on those very same handlebars. It's like a scene from an olive oil advert. Luca Scinto, Zanini's similarly lantern-jawed teammate, trundles through, laughing as usual. Max told me a good story about Scinto, who he often trains with.

Scinto is out on a training ride with a pal when, ever the joker, he decides to have a little fun with his young friend's accoutrements. Reaching deftly into his companion's jersey pocket without disturbing him, Scinto manages to guide the fellow's sandwich to freedom. As they carry on riding and chatting, he carefully unwraps the morsel and begins to munch away. With a frown, the other chap says, 'Isn't it a bit early to be eating?'

'Oh, don't worry,' he replies, 'I'll have mine later.' It's only then that the companion realises he's been duped into losing his lunch. 'Hey!' he laughs, reaching into Scinto's pocket for quick retribution. His fingers latch on to the big man's cap, and he tugs it out and hurls it on to the passing tarmac.

'No!' yells Scinto, as the little *cappellino* hits the floor with a distinctly un-cotton-like smash. For before he'd left the house that morning, Luca Scinto had wrapped up his tiny, brand-new, top-of-the-range Nokia in that very cap.

At the feed station, where I am helping Adrian hand out *musettes* in between phone calls to Mavic, Principia and Look to sort out bike kit, Sean pulls up in the Laguna behind the race.

'John, take the Espace and go to the hospital in Vicenza. Matt's crashed – looks like his collarbone has gone. Ada, you'd better come in with me,' and off they speed.

After a search of the local environs, I find Vicenza, then the hospital, and finally Stephens himself. It is indeed the collarbone. However, on the plus side, the hospital is immaculate, the race ambulance brought him here quickly, and they've already x-rayed him. After a short wait, the doctor comes in to give Matt the not-so-bad news – off the bike for three weeks, wear this brace to keep it straight. Seeing as Andrea was now five months pregnant, heading home for a while was a blessing in disguise for the Stephens household. I phoned Sean to let him know what was happening, and to find out how the others had got on.

'At the hospital,' he said.

'Yes,' I replied, 'we're at the hospital.'

'No, we're at the hospital.'

'What?'

'I'm with Ben at the hospital in Padova. He crashed about 10 km after Matt – looks like his collarbone too.'

Good grief.

Ben wasn't so lucky – the hospital in Padova made the worst inner-city NHS Trust place look like a scene out of a BUPA advert. What a dump. What's more, the team had to move on to the next of our clutch of races, so it was decided that I would stay behind in Padova to sort things out.

There was worse to follow for Ben. In a masterful display of tact, timing and diplomacy, Sean picked that evening to tell the young Aussie that he was not part of the team's plans for 2001.

In contrast to Matt's quick assessment and treatment, the hospital wouldn't let Ben leave that night. They'd strapped and bandaged his left arm to his side, and said that because he may have banged his head he would have to stay in for supervision, and they would reassess the damage in the morning. He was left on his own in a room that looked like it was in the middle of redecoration, or possibly demolition. Five empty beds surrounded his one, with paint peeling off the walls all round. As for supervision, I didn't see a nurse, doctor or orderly the whole evening; the place was deserted.

With Ben at a low, Matt and I wondered how we could cheer him up.

'I know! How about a cheeky McDonald's?'

Ben had never been the most crusading of vegetarians, and he wolfed down a Big Mac one-handed with a look of delight on his face. I took off the Groucho glasses-and-moustache disguise, the Homburg hat and the big overcoat I'd worn to enter the forbidden temple under the golden arches to bring back the loot.

Ben's folks were on holiday in the Alps, and we managed to get word to them that he was hurt, so they drove down to the hospital the next day. After putting Matt on a flight back to England from Venice, I headed to the hospital again to see them all. Mum and Dad were very pleased to be with their son, but increasingly frustrated at the lack of action in the hospital. I finally tracked down a doctor who said he wanted to give Ben a brainscan, but it wouldn't be until the next day.

When I gave Ben the bad news, he burst into tears. 'That's what they said yesterday! I can't stay here another night,' he sobbed. 'I didn't even land on my head – there's not a mark on it.' It was true, he was there because he'd broken his collarbone, and they'd done all they were going to do for that.

I took a deep breath and said, 'Get your stuff together, we're out of here.' Back at Lucifer's Hotel in Monte del Terme, the four of us went out to a pizzeria to discuss Ben's future. As we were waiting for the *gelati* to arrive, my phone rang. It was Sean.

'I've just had the Veneto race organiser on the phone – where's Ben?'

'He's here with me, we left the hospital this afternoon.'

'You'd better get back there – they've got the police out looking for you.'

Jesus Christ, now we were wanted felons for our escape from Colditz. Ben and I hopped into the team car and drove back to the hospital. The ward where he had been held captive was across the road from the main part of the hospital, and was all locked up. We walked all around it, finding chains around door handles and padlocks everywhere. God knows what would have happened if they'd had to evacuate in an emergency. I walked the half-mile to the main reception to give us up, but nobody knew what I was talking about, so we threw in the towel and went back to the hotel.

The next morning I returned and patched things up with the hospital. The doctor who had refused to let Ben leave originally took a very dim view of our bid for freedom, but he got down off his high horse fairly abruptly when I told him about all the locked doors I'd encountered the night before. We were allowed to leave Padova with our criminal records unblemished. Or, at least, no worse than they'd been before.

It was a shame about Ben. Whilst he had not been our most successful rider, everybody agreed about how talented he was. After all, you could hardly describe him as wasted talent when he was still only 21. I felt he was worth another season, especially after we had invested two years in him. To let him go now seemed like a waste.

However, Sean had a different view. He felt that despite Ben's obvious class, his attitude was wrong, and his application poor. For six weeks or so, Ben would be the model pro, training hard, eating carefully, preparing wisely and racing well. For the next six weeks, he would show no interest or motivation, sitting at home watching TV and eating junk food.

'I thought that if he could achieve a little more consistency in his approach, Ben would make a really good rider,' explained Sean. 'But with no results to speak of after two years with us, I had to make a harsh decision, and that was to let him go.'

Sean's management style was to say to his riders, 'You're all professionals, that's why you're here. You know what I expect of you, let's go and do it.' This philosophy was more than welcomed by the more experienced riders who thrived on the maturity and trust placed in them. It helped bond our special team spirit that meant so much within the McCartney squad. For younger riders, though, it was perhaps less effective, and it is interesting that Ben, and Spencer before him, felt that Keith Lambert's more hands-on style of management got the best out of them.

From Italy, it was a long trip north to Belgium. As I drove along the beautiful *autostrada* that bypasses Turin and heads up into the Alps and the Frejus Tunnel, my phone rang. It was Matt.

'I've got some news for you, Johnny boy. Andrea's had a baby boy, Josh, this morning.' I was delighted, yet confused – I felt embarrassed at having got the dates wrong, I didn't think Andrea was due until Christmas time.

'No mate, you're all right,' Matt confirmed. 'He's ten weeks early.' What a mixture of emotions must have been rushing through Matt and Andrea. They had been trying for a baby for some time, and lost two at an early stage. Now their joy was tempered by a terrible fear and worry for this tiny, tiny man. 'He's two pounds,' said Matt. 'I had him on the palm of my hand. He's in an incubator now, they say he's doing well and fighting strong, but it's too early to say.' Matt was disguising it well, but I could hear the pain in his voice. 'That's great news!' I said cheerfully, as tears began to flood down my face. Bike racing? Bouncing cheques? Everything else in life suddenly seemed like a cheap seaside postcard in comparison to Josh's difficult start in the world.

Ada, Topper and I stopped off at a Hotel Campanile near Dijon en route. 'Do you have anything without meat or fish apart from the salad?'

'Non.'

'Could you make us an omelette please?'

'Non.'

It was so good to be back in enlightened France.

Max was riding brilliantly. Consistently our top performer in the second half of the season, he was very keen to perform well at the Olympics and at the World Championships for Great Britain. He was getting some great support from Mirko Puglioli, a chirpy Italian we had picked up as a *stagiere* until the end of the season. The *stagiere* system is a chance for pro teams to give younger riders a trial in the hope that they will find a permanent place in the team in the future. In Mirko's case, his willingness, positive attitude and good results were a passport to a proper berth in the team for 2001. Eleventh in the tough GP Fourmies French Cup event was his best ride, but he was always there or thereabouts.

At Paris–Brussels, he was there again alongside Max.

SCIANDRI NEARING HIS PEAK

Great Britain's Max Sciandri of the Linda McCartney Pro Cycling Team is running into his very best form with perfect timing. In his last week of racing before leaving for Sydney and the Olympics, Max turned in a great performance at yesterday's Paris–Brussels classic.

'I certainly had the legs today,' said Max of the epic 250 km race across Northern France and Belgium.

Twice within the last 20 km it looked as though Max had got into winning moves. After his first effort was recaptured by what was left of 200-odd starters, Max went again immediately, in the company of Michele Bartoli, Leon Van Bon, Arven Piziks, Roman Vainsteins and a few other luminaries. 'I looked around at the group, saw we were all working, and thought, "This is it." I could not believe it when I looked over my shoulder and saw the bunch coming back up to us. There must have only been 10 km to go.'

Riding at the front of a race of this quality over the last 50 km is easier said than done, and Max's constant contributions to the action will have done his confidence a power of good. A murmur went around the pressroom as he smoothly cruised on to Bartoli's wheel that could be translated as, 'Sciandri is back to his best'.

In the end, it was Bartoli's Mapei sprinter teammate Max Van Heeswijk who rocketed out of the bunch to take the victor's bouquet by around five bike lengths. Linda McCartney's Mirko Puglioli had also survived the mammoth distance and ran in alongside Max.

Ireland's Ciaran Power also rode magnificently, in what was

the longest race of this quality that he has ever finished. He rode at the front all day, successfully making every consecutive split in the *peloton* until exhaustion and the excessive speed from the front eventually put paid to his efforts with just 15 km to go. Tailed off by the leaders, he nevertheless finished proudly, and will be delighted with his upturn in form, also nicely timed for Australia.

John Deering
Linda McCartney Pro Cycling Team

After three races in Belgium and northern France, it was time to head home.

'Make sure you've got enough diesel when you're in Belgium,' warned Julian on the phone from Toulouse, 'there's a crisis on down here and all the garages are shut.' The fuel blockades that would shortly hit Britain had already bitten hard in the south of France. We filled up all the vehicles after the finish in Belgium, and bought as many jerrycans as we could carry. Sean wedged the large red containers into the back of team car 2, driven by me, and we headed back down the road towards Paris, straight into some major traffic. We laughed and sang in the car, spirits high . . . with the scent of diesel rising. Matt De Canio and Ciaran Power had become good mates over the last few weeks, and they in particular were chorusing loudly, and very nearly harmoniously, in the Laguna. My other passenger was the quieter Welshman, Huw Pritchard. He was over with the 'A' Team for some good racing experience, and enjoying the trip.

'Huw,' I asked as the smell of diesel grew ever stronger, 'just have a quick glance in the back and check those cans are OK, will you?' He got up on to his knees and peered over the back seat into the estate boot.

'Oh fuck.'

Of the eight cans, one was standing upright. The other seven were now only half full. I reckon there were about 35 litres of diesel swashing around the boot of the car. We were stuck in a traffic jam somewhere between Brussels and Paris, with three cyclists off their heads on noxious fumes and a car awash with diesel. Needless to say, Sean and the occupants of team car 1 found this hilarious, and laughed their heads off. 'Bastaaaaaards!' I yelled.

The riders flew home from CDG, Craig and I spent the night shampooing and hosing out the car, but it still reeked to high heaven when I drove it all the way south the next day. In fact, the last time I opened that car door was that Christmas, and I reeled back holding my nose as the pungent odour of diesel spilled three months previously still filled the vehicle. Now, two years on, I don't know who owns it, what colour it is or where it resides, but I reckon I could still identify it pretty quickly if I got a sniff inside.

It was a long drive back to Toulouse, with lots of time to think. It was clear that the team had lost their faith in Julian, but were incredibly loyal to Sean. They were also very positive about Stevo and the new guys he was trying to bring in. There were three excellent Spaniards he had lined up: Miguel Martin Perdiguero, a seriously quick finisher from the soon-to-be-defunct Vitalicio Seguros team; Juan Carlos Dominguez, also from Vitalicio, and a master of the one-week stage races so popular in Spain; and Iñigo Cuesta, like Neil himself a trojan from Once who was ready to spread his wings under Stevo's guidance.

Cycling is a highly unstable business. A professional cycling team is not like a football club, founded 100 years ago and kept alive even in the throes of bankruptcy by loyal followers who have grown up loving their club like a member of the family. Cycling teams are here today, gone tomorrow. A major sponsor stays in the sport for about three years on average, some a lot less. Long-term benefactors like Mapei, Kelme, Rabobank and Banesto are hard to find. Even with these companies and the great marketing benefits they promise cycling has brought them, you can bet your life that the driving force behind their commitment to a team is that the man at the top is a cycling nut who loves being involved. Even finding smaller sponsors was unbelievably difficult, as we were finding out.

Having ridden for myriad teams over the years, all facing the same problems as us, our riders were only too aware of what life is like at the thin end of the wedge. Payment problems and a team's financial difficulties were nothing new to them, that's why they didn't just walk away, they realised that this is the sort of shit that goes on from time to time, and it's best to roll with it and come out the other side.

We were already planning for next year, so it couldn't be too bad. The most logical explanation for all our money troubles was a cashflow problem – money going out before it had come in. The worst possible scenario was that the team would fold and we'd all go home. I thought that if it came to that I could handle it, but it wouldn't come to that.

I went to see Julian to talk things over. Tracie was there too, and I told them both that there was deep, deep unease in the team and everybody would like to know what was going on. He explained that there had been a problem with our regular payments from Linda McCartney, but told me he was sure it would be OK. By the end of our talk I felt much happier. I still had a few doubts, but was sure that everything was going to be all right.

Despite it being pretty unknown in the UK, only the World Cup events of Milan–San Remo and the Tour of Lombardy are considered bigger one-day races than the Giro del Lazio. Max had been trying to win it for ten years; its glorious finish outside the Colosseum in Rome was his favourite in all of cycling. On 16 September 2000, he got his wish. After 200 km of scrapping with the cream of Italian cycling, Max outsprinted men-of-the-moment Francesco Casagrande and Sergio Barbero to take one of his best-ever wins.

I called Sean on his mobile from the *service course* in Cornebarrieu. He was driving back to the hotel from the finish in Rome, Max in the passenger seat still clutching his winner's bouquet, a great day for both of them.

'Congratulations, boss!' I shouted.

'Thanks, mate, it was a superb win, he's really deserved it the way he's been going lately. Want to speak to him?'

'Yes please,' I waited as Sean passed the phone to Max.

'*Pronto*, Max?'

'*Ciao,* John.'

'Fantastic result, mate, well done; I know how much this race means to you.'

'Yeah, thanks, John, it was great. Listen, John – do you know what the fuck is going on with my money?'

Chapter 10: Listen To What The Man Said

Back in Surrey, my friends at Sigma Sport had struck a deal with Julian. Ian Whittingham explains:

'Julian asked me if he could borrow about £10,000 from the shop as a short-term loan, just for a few days, to cover some payments he had to make. In return, he would over-order on the components for the team's new bikes, so we could have some of it.'

Under the terms of the Linda McCartney sponsorship deal with Shimano, all the gears, brakes, etc., for the team bikes were supplied at a cost significantly less than trade price, so this was a good deal for Sigma, who could sell the components through the shop with a much better margin than usual. At the time I knew nothing about the exchange.

'The few days turned into a few weeks, until we were close to the time when we would be getting the Shimano stuff anyway,' continued Ian. 'As we were spending roughly the same amount on that as the cash we'd already lent the team, I agreed to turn the loan into a payment for the stuff we were expecting.'

Clearly there was a breakdown of communication somewhere, as for one reason or another Sigma has not yet been repaid; in money or components.

At around the same time, Julian told me of an interesting and surprising development that affected me directly. 'You know that I'm really happy with the work that you've done for the team,' he told me, 'and I want to continue that and expand it for next year. I've taken on Denis Lancaster, so there will be two of you to do it.'

I was a little taken aback, as I had heard nothing about this. I had known Denis for a couple of years; he had been a sportswriter and sub-editor at the *Express*, running a cycling column that had run many stories about the team. At first I suppose I selfishly felt a bit undermined by his appointment, but when I weighed it up it made sense. If we were going to be racing at more than one place at the same time as was intended, one of us could travel with each half of the squad. We got on very well and shared similar views on how the job should be done.

I believe that when Denis joined the team he also invested some money in it, but I don't know the precise details. Denis had recently sold his house and moved to Italy to be with his new girlfriend.

A well-respected sports lawyer who represented a number of people in a variety of sports also allegedly invested a significant sum. We have no idea if other people were lending the team money, unaware of our existing debts, but it's possible that further loans covered our wages that autumn. Even Terry Clark, Julian's dad, claimed that he had been bailing out the team for some time. Terry, who owns a haulage business in east London, once hinted to me he had helped out with our wages.

The team was incurring big debts to cover existing problems. We had to do something about them before next season to cover them. Luckily, Julian was not short of ideas. I believe that the plan was to use all the excellent publicity from 2000 to pull in at least two big-name sponsors who would shoulder the majority of the team costs, with a bit left over to pay back the people who had unwittingly bailed us out in 2000. Linda McCartney Foods, under the auspices of MPL, Sir Paul's company, wanted to take more of a back seat while Heinz, as the manufacturers and distributors of the food, seemed to be benefiting most from the marketing. MPL were willing to let the team continue to use Linda's name and consolidate the excellent image we had made, but were not prepared to be the main contributors any longer; they saw that as Heinz's responsibility.

So, what to do? At that stage, I was aware that we needed more money coming in, but I wasn't sure what role McCartney would play in 2001.

One option on Julian's desk was to take up Dr Oxenberg's interest in the team. Julian said that the good doctor was no longer interested in becoming a sub-sponsor of the team – he wanted to buy the whole kit and caboodle off Julian. While this had its obvious attractions, removing the worries building over Julian's head, he was loath to relinquish the reins just when it appeared that three years' graft was showing signs of paying off. Though the new deal would involve Julian staying on as a salaried general manager, the team would no longer be his and his alone.

The arrangement was shrouded in mystery for us then, and remains so to this day. What did the proposed buy-out entail? What was Oxenberg's business plan? Whatever the answers to these questions, the upshot was clear: the deal was not going to happen.

We kept on piling into companies and hitting them with proposals. Julian would make contact, I would write a proposal and he would follow it up. That autumn we approached AGF Insurance and AON Insurance; Guinness, Murphy's and Beamish; Nivea, Gillette and Canesten; Lloyds, Abbey National and Commonwealth Banks; Qantas, British Airways and Ryanair; TNT, DHL and UPS . . . the list was endless. We got through to the making contact and talking stage with upwards of 60 companies, and literally hundreds were hit with proposals.

Julian was good at this sort of thing; after all, it had been his work that had started the whole thing rolling a couple of years before, and the atmosphere at the *service course* was electric with industry and optimism. Our offices were split by a little corridor and we would be shouting snippets of news and responses through to each other all the time. Lisa, Ciaran's fiancée, would be sat in my office, diligently ploughing through the thousands of requests we got for photographs, caps, jerseys and autographs, reciprocating wherever possible. Our new French mechanic, Arnaud, was buzzing around the main service area, building toolracks or welding wheelracks onto the wall with his equally determined father.

Life in Toulouse was as good as it gets. Our social scene had widened now that we had become figures of interest to the local English-speaking community. This was a sizeable bunch, stemming originally from the British Aerospace contingent based around the *aerogare* at Blagnac, but now encompassing all sorts of add-on industries like shops, bars, employment and accommodation agencies. Though there were a large proportion of Costa-del-Dickhead Brits-on-the-piss types around – 'Aye, us've bin 'ere seven and twenty years, don't speak a bloody word o' French, and bloody proud of't, too,' there were plenty of people like us too, keen to embrace France and the culture of the *sud-ouest*, but always pleased to meet folk similar to themselves.

The epicentre of British activity is Pibrac, a thriving suburban village just beyond the airport from the centre of Toulouse that is fast becoming an English enclave. The easy thing to do is to get a job at BAe, move to Pibrac, send your kids to the euphemistically titled International School of Toulouse – it's more Middle England than Buckinghamshire – go for a pint in The Bell and never have to speak to a French person as long as you live. The friendly nature of the locals means that you won't have to run the gauntlet of prejudice or disapproval that might meet, say, a French family moving to England and making no effort whatsoever to mix with the natives. Pibrac was indeed an excellent landing place for us when we began to arrive in late '99, but by early 2000 most of us were keen to sample something a little less like what we had left behind. I had found a great place for Louise, Kit and me in Aussonne, then Julian and Tracie bought a place just down the road. On a bike-borne scout round one morning, he found a terrific little industrial unit that would become our *service course* in the next village, Cornebarrieu, two minutes from the airport. Ben lived with a BAe guy called Richard Neville in a superb old barn conversion attached to a chateau a couple of klicks east, while the McKenzies and the Powers preferred the thriving cosmopolitan buzz of central Toulouse. Country life isn't for everybody, as Spencer and Melissa certainly found to their cost when they moved into a flat in the outpost village of Pelleport, where even the tumbleweed gets lonely – beautiful, but deathly quiet for Melissa when Spencer was away racing. Their move to the slightly nearer village of Brax brought about a marginal improvement on their view of France, but their overall impressions will never be great. Matt sampled life at the chateau with Ben, then slotted into bedroom No. 2 at the luxury Deering pad in Aussonne after the lady of the house had departed.

Craig sorted himself a really nice small apartment in Colomiers, one step in towards the city from Pibrac, and probably one of the smallest places in the world to have such a successful sports club as their rugby team. Colomiers remains, to my admittedly limited knowledge, the only place in France where you still have to give way to people *coming on* to roundabouts. There's nothing to tell you this, exactly: you're just meant to know. Cue lots of hilarious incidents involving vacant foreigners driving happily and obliviously around whilst locals turn a sort of apoplectic blue with rage. In addition, Colomiers is one of those newtown-style places that seem riddled with roundabouts, amplifying the problem as much as can be possible. This surely must be to the ultimate satisfaction of those who decided to stick to this plan when the rest of the world had decided it was a bad idea. We developed our own plan to combat this evil – whenever passing the 'Colomiers' sign, you would have to keep saying 'Colomiers, I am in Colomiers' out loud until the corresponding sign that signified the end of the town was safely behind you. Must have been a nightmare for Craig.

My best friends in Toulouse remain the excellent bunch of teachers from the International School that I became entwined with that year. I cherish my friendships with Liz, Sophie, Megan, Peter Flynn and all their crowd as the abiding good thing that came out of our own little 'Year in Provence' (it's not far) and will call them friends until the day I die.

Flynn and I developed a taste for going to Toulouse FC on a Saturday night. Their stadium is built upon an island in the Garonne in downtown Toulouse, a beautiful piece of modern French architecture dreamt up for the 1998 World Cup. Our first visit was undertaken with the dispassionate curiosity of foreign onlookers – ooh, it's only a fiver to get in; lovely ground, eh? You don't get many away fans, do you? Ooh, they don't like a tackle, do they? Within a fortnight we were yelling, '*Tolosa! Tolosa!*' in the vernacular old Occitaine, chanting the name of our hero, the Colombian Victor Bonilla, and calling the referee a bald twat. Just like home. I remember leaping to my feat in the last quarter of a particularly fraught relegation battle, shouting in 100-miles-an-hour West Londonese, 'Offside? *Offside*? How can he possibly be offside when he's behind the ball? Have you even *seen* a game of football before, ref, you stupid bastard?' Reaching the end of my rant I realised that there were a good couple of dozen bemused and astonished Toulousain faces turned up towards me from the surrounding seats as Flynn pulled ashamedly at my trouser leg. I sat down sheepishly, my face now red due to embarrassment rather than the anger that had got me up on my feet in the first place.

Our support didn't seem to spur them on too much. They were relegated from the top division, relegated again immediately for some dodgy financial dealings, then their beautiful little stadium – *la petite Wembley* – was seriously damaged by the huge chemical factory explosion that rocked Toulouse in the autumn of 2001. It remains closed for the foreseeable future, no great hardship to the football-watching public of Toulouse who had voted with their feet en masse to the team's ignominious departure from the top flight anyway.

The explosion has crippled Toulouse in the short term, and affected the lives of everybody living there. Though initial fears that the blast was linked to the atrocities in New York and Washington on 11 September were refuted, plenty of mystery remains about how such a catastrophic event could have occurred. Everything around the factory on the southern fringes of the city was flattened, while virtually no glass withstood the shock on that side of town. Le Bikini, a great little venue where we had seen Frank Black deliver a masterclass in twenty-first-century rock 'n' roll, finally succumbed to the fate so many great acts had threatened: it had its roof blown off.

That morning, Ciaran had been taking things rather easy after an end-of-season heavy night on the tiles with Big Mat's Jay Sweet. The boys were up, but barely. The Playstation was taking up what little of their attention was still available, and the metal shutters used throughout Ciaran and Lisa's apartment block were yet to be raised on their flat alone, the neighbours having all trotted off dutifully for work. This explained why the enormous bang that occurred halfway through the morning shattered every glass door in that frontage of flats except the Powers'.

At the school in Pibrac, maybe 10 km away, all the classroom doors swung silently open as the shockwave spread out around the Haute Garonne. Down at Magnus Backstedt and Stuart O'Grady's places even further out in Muret, people stopped in the street as the ground shook beneath them.

Amazingly, only 29 people were killed in the explosion, but it has changed the appearance of the city we know and love – beyond recognition in some parts.

I guess it's fair to say that the people who took to our new lifestyle most readily were the Clarks, the Powers and me. Julian and Tracie made friends easily, especially through Oliver, who was by now a bright and precocious five-year-old, in danger of turning into a wrinkled old prune with all the time he spent with me in their lovely pool. Lisa loved Toulouse too, finding it a pleasant surprise after the contrast of drab and less welcoming Nantes, where Ciaran had spent a year as an amateur. I thought it was the most wonderful place I could imagine living: an ancient city with a beating, cosmopolitan heart; the beautiful rolling roads of Gers a short ride west from our homes and the majesty of the Pyrenees only an hour south in the car.

The McKenzies liked it too, having found a very smart apartment beside the Canal du Midi not far from the main station right in town, but they pined a little for the friends and family they had left behind in Ghent, a town they had grown to love in the same way I was taking to Toulouse. Craig was another who felt that Belgium was the place to be for anyone living the cycling life. It's no accident that they have gravitated back north to Flanders since the McCartney days.

Surprisingly for many, Sean only came to Toulouse a handful of times during our entire tenure. Like Craig, Sean went to almost every single race, meaning he was on the road almost constantly, so the need for him to move his base was lessened. Furthermore, unlike Craig, Sean had a happily expanding family at home in Sussex who weren't quite ready to up sticks and move out – Pippa's third baby, Bathsheba, was born that summer, and she already had her hands full enough with their two boys, so the support of their parents near to home was important.

He was on the road constantly throughout August and September, as the team were scudding round Italy on a mass of races all the way through to the Olympics and the World Championships. In addition to Veneto and Lazio, they had been to Coppa Sabatini, Giro dell'Emilia, Milano–Vignola, Coppa Placci, Trofeo Melinda . . . the list went on and on.

Shortly before Max, Ciaran and Bjornar were to head off to Sydney for the Olympics, Julian seemed to strike gold. Using our bright new image, squeaky-clean reputation and the lure of famous Australians making it big in Europe, he had all but sealed a deal with the South Australian wine giants Jacob's Creek to be co-sponsors of the team for the next two years. Everybody was delighted, not least Sean and Stevo, who had been working their butts off to pull the riders and programme together for 2001. With the £1.7 million we hoped would soon be tucked away in the bank from Jacob's Creek, we were confident that it could all be paid for. And there was more to come, we were sure – Julian had been beavering away on a deal with Jaguar cars that was looking more and more likely each day.

Plans for the next year were taking shape. The programme would be based around the Tours of Italy in the spring and Spain in the autumn, with all the week-long stage races in both those countries in between. There would be room for plenty of racing in France too, but we would go to the Belgium and Dutch semi-classics less often. The World Cup was no longer an immediate aim – we felt more confidence in finding results in the stage races. Sean would run the Italian operation whilst Stevo would take charge of things in Spain. The *service course* in Cornebarrieu would remain our home, with a second base in the Basque Country housing the vehicles and support staff we would need for races south of the Pyrenees. We didn't plan on the Tour de France, but if a sniff of an entry was possible, commercial advantages dictated we would throw everything at it. In the meantime, our official line was that 2002 was our target for the big one.

The rider line-up was finalised. Staying on with increased salaries from 2000 would be Max Sciandri, David McKenzie, Matt Stephens, Tayeb

Braikia, Ciaran Power, Bjornar Vestol and new boy Mirko Puglioli. Joining them would be Iñigo Cuesta, Miguel Martin Perdiguero and Juan Carlos Dominguez. The Australian arm of the team was being strengthened, with Marcel Gono and Pete Rogers joining Macca. Home sensibilities were addressed by bringing in British Champion John Tanner, former junior world pursuit champion Bradley Wiggins and our returning hero Russell Downing. Even more English-speaking prowess was unveiled when we revealed that 1998 World Junior Road Race Champion Mark Scanlon would be coming from Ireland, and there would be staunch support from Czech Ondrej Fadrny, Russian Sergei Lelekin and Colombia's Marlon Perez.

Max and Bjornar both showed well in the Olympic Road Race, making the front group of 21 with 30 km remaining. Unfortunately, they (and everybody else) had come upon that irrefutable force of nature, the late-season Jan Ullrich. If they ever have the Tour de France in September, he'll piss it, as he will have had nine months to digest all the fizzy pop and sausage rolls he downed at Christmas instead of the usual seven. When he launched his second acceleration with a lap and a half of the circuit left, it was 'see yer later' time for all and sundry except his Telekom mates Kloden and Vinokourov. Even a frantic tandem chase by Bartoli and Bettini made no impression, the two of them looking incredulously up at the big video screen as they passed it, knowing they were giving it everything yet getting nowhere. This time, even Armstrong had to concede to a stronger man, and Max was happy to be rolling in with the bunch sprinting for 14th. Ciaran was a proud finisher in 74th, nearly six minutes down after 240 draining kilometres. Bjornar eventually came home another minute later, absolutely exhausted from the effort of going with Ullrich's first attack.

Max's season wasn't quite finished, as he had one eye on the World Championships in Plouay. Principia had built him a special super-light black bike for the Olympics, but in the end he had decided to use his normal team issue yellow Rex, because the course contained just the one 'power' climb, more suited to the stiffer yet slightly heavier bike. The Worlds course in Brittany was a different matter, though, difficult, rolling 'heavy' roads meaning that the light climber's bike would indeed get a run out.

Before he could get out of New South Wales, though, our man would run into a problem. Out training with his GB teammate David Millar, the duo were disturbed by one of those Australian truck drivers unaware that cyclists even exist. He didn't quite manage to make contact, but Dave's evasive action was enough to send Max crashing to the ground. When I saw him in Brittany two weeks later, he was quite a sight.

'Hey, John, check this out,' Max said, dropping his drawers. His left hip was the epicentre of the biggest bruise I've ever seen, cascading down round his bony hip and totally enveloping his bollocks in a frightening recreation of a medieval painting, warning the passing peasant that hell hath many horrors to torment a man. On the hip itself sat an attractive sack of skin holding a gallon or two of the fluid that had built up. 'I've had the doctor suck it off with a syringe twice now,' winced Max. 'It hurts,' he added unnecessarily. 'I might need it drawing off again before the race tomorrow. He's given me a syringe – can you do it for me?'

'Ooh, look at that up there, Max, a shooting star,' I stammered, racing for the safety of my own little room.

Julian and I had driven up to Brittany to meet Stevo and tie up some contracts. Neil brought Perdiguero and Dominguez's lawyer to meet Julian and finalise details of their contracts, whilst we also met Russell Downing at the GB camp and got Bjornar to put a pen to his renewed contract.

Neil was there as manager for the Australian team, and at dinner the night before the big race he told us that Scott Sunderland was getting under his skin. 'You'd think all the crashes he's had over the years would've slowed him up, but I think it's just affected his brain – he thinks he's something really special,' complained Stevo. 'We had a look at the course today, and he made me go back for another look at the finish. The finish! The only time he's going to need to know anything about the finish is how to find our pit area when he packs.'

I took my hat off to both of them the following day, when the resurgent Sunderland finished a breathtaking seventh in the same time as the new World Champion, Romans Vainsteins, with Max an excellent 18th in the same group. Stevo ate more humble pie than one would have thought possible, totally giving it up for Sunderland's excellent ride. 'Still don't want him in my team, mind,' he added with a smile.

Dinner that night was a tremendous affair, a posh restaurant in Lorient playing host to a party of Julian, Max, Max's brother-in-law, Russell Downing, myself and Jim Ochowicz, the man who had been Max and Sean's old boss at Motorola. Jim seemed to be an expert on a hell of a lot of things, so most of the time we listened while he talked; not a bad idea when our team was largely based upon a model of his own. He was also keen to educate us on the subject of wine, and convert us to the joys of St Emilion. There was time to extol the values of a fresh fish diet too, slightly dubious ground for the vegetarians.

The fish question was one we were often asked, and I usually skirted round it. The basic rule was that it was up to riders and staff as to where they wished to draw their individual line on vegetarianism – it didn't bother me as I didn't really like fish anyway. We made a point of not eating fish when we were away at races, just for the reason that it could easily have become a rod for our own backs. Other than that, I think more guys than not enjoyed fish. Julian in particular would always make short work of a tuna steak. As for me and my philistine's palate that didn't take to seafood, it was an ethical decision I never had to face. Hoorah!

That night, Russ and I looked on in a mixture of wonder, awe and plain disgust as the others slurped their way through a tray of oysters, prodding them first for signs of life before tipping them squealing down their gullets. OK, so they weren't actually squealing, but I'm trying to tell a story here, all right?

Another good thing to come out of the World Championships was Richey Wooles. He was working for the GB team as a *soigneur*, and impressed everybody, especially Max. The problems we had suffered with *soigneurs* made it a must to snap up a good one whenever we could, so we checked his availability with the team manager, John Herety, then made him an offer for 2001 which he accepted. He would soon become a resident of Lot du Castelets, Aussonne, and I have to say that the place never looked tidier. Fancy having your own personal *soigneur* clearing up after you? What a life.

Julian and I drove down the lovely autoroute that runs from Toulouse to Biarritz in the shadow of the high Pyrenees to meet Stevo for a day's business in the Basque Country. We stopped off en route to admire the motorway services' fantastic shiny sculpture that celebrates the Tour de France's passage through the mountains, wondering what the chances were of finding something similar at Heston Services. We don't even get an 'Angel of the North' round there; it might prove a danger to low-flying aircraft that close to Heathrow.

On the way down, Julian explained that the deal with Jaguar was near completion too, so we could press on with our kit designs for 2001. The colours were to be predominantly green and gold for two reasons: firstly, we felt that our 2000 strip, nice as it was, was extremely hard to discern in the bunch, especially from the following team cars, as everybody's shorts appeared very similar. Secondly, we wanted to play on the Australian side of our image for maximum PR value, and linking Jacob's Creek with the national colours seemed like a good idea, especially as gold had been established as our main colour since the beginning of the team.

We spent the morning with the engaging trio of people running things at Etxe-Ondo, the Basque specialists who were designing and making the new strip. Paco was the main man, and drove the thing with his wife. A younger guy, Ramon, who spoke excellent English, was our main contact. They had made Once and Banesto clothing for many years, but the big bucks of some of the cycle clothing giants had squeezed them out. They were now supplying the local favourites, the Basque team Euskatel with their distinctive fluoro orange kit, and the quality of their gear was absolutely second to none. We had enjoyed good quality stuff from Giordana in 2000, but the feeling was that we were too far down the pecking order there to be able to get the best service – Cofidis, Mercury and US Postal (their Nike stuff was ghosted by Giordana) all had more clout than us.

Paco turned out to be a real character. Looking like a tougher Claudio

Rainieri, 50-ish, hard as nails and as passionate about cycling as any Basque, he had ridden training rides for many years with the Once boys when Neil had been there.

'One day we were out, about ten of us, all Once riders and Paco,' remembered Stevo. 'Everyone was chatting and joking except Paco, who was deadly serious. He had a point to prove to all the pros, you see. As we rode past him, one of us delicately flicked the quick release up on his back brake. Then, in turn, as we passed him going through and off, each of us gave a little quiet twist on his brake adjuster. When it was tight enough to be almost brushing the rim, we got on quite a steep climb, like you get a lot of round here. We flipped his quick release back on and it just jammed his back brake on; he had to stop and sort it out. We were all roaring of course, but he was cursing and came flying after us. Not long after he had caught us, Johan Bruyneel (now Lance's director at USPS) tried it again, but of course Paco was wise to us by now, and he angrily slapped Bruyneel's hand away. Only problem was, he hit Johan's handlebars, Johan hit the road on his knee, and was out for six months!' Even though the tale was related in English for our benefit, Paco hung his head in mock shame at the old story.

Joking over, he turned his attentions to the extremely serious business of designing a cycling jersey. This involved closing his eyes so tight that his face screwed up into a Keith Richards impression, placing the fingers of one hand on his temples to aid deep thought, whilst drumming the fingers of the other hand on the table top. Equally imperative was total silence from everyone else in the room, virtually impossible for Julian and I who were close to pissing ourselves at this fantastic tableau. Stevo had seen it all before and had wisely buried his head deep in some engrossing laptop display, only too aware that we were desperately trying to catch his eye. Paco's wife and Ramon looked as if they saw this performance five times a day – let's face it, they probably did. For a few weeks afterwards, whenever I asked Julian a question, he would go into his Paco impression for a few seconds before the laughter we managed to suppress that day kicked in.

With much enjoyable animated discussion and input from everyone, we came away with a beautiful kit. It was a beautiful rich evergreen and gold, and the cloth was to be made with Linda's signature actually woven into the pattern of the fabric. Ramon took us on a factory tour, loading us up with the most gorgeous samples and freebies of gear as we went round. He also explained that all their pro-team kit is made in two ranges of sizes: professional and retail. XXXL in professional roughly equates to L in their retail sizes, giving you some idea of just how thin your average pro is. Either that, or he was just trying to buff up my ego after giving me an XXXL pair of shorts.

On the way to lunch, Julian broached the subject of Stevo's fantastic and timeless hairstyle, the Mullet of Ages. 'My wife's sister cuts it,' explains the Aussie. 'She always says to me, "Same as usual, Neil, little bit off the front, little bit off the back?" and I say yeah.'

'Next time,' I suggested helpfully, 'why don't you say "Little bit off the front, whole fucking carpet-load off the back?"' We laughed more than him. He wasn't averse to having the piss taken out of him, but I don't think Neil would count it among his favourite hobbies. That's a shame when you're with two London-ish boys who know no other way to make conversation.

'Nobody would recognise me then,' he replied after a couple of minutes, not unreasonably.

'Mate, that horse face would get you recognised anywhere. Even in a stable,' he was told.

In the end, people drifted off in different directions as their seasons finished at different times. The Christmas party we'd talked about never really happened; it's a tricky operation when some people who have become friends are leaving, and people you don't know are joining. In the end, we had a big Christmas do combined with a birthday bash for Peter Flynn at my place, but by that time most of the team personnel had departed for a winter break. Julian, Tracie, Oliver and Matthew came, Ciaran and Lisa had a great time, while Arnaud and Richey enjoyed meeting new friends, but the vast majority of revellers were teachers from the school, drinking as only teachers know how.

My folks arrived for Christmas and we enjoyed our meat-free Christmas dinner in the conservatory with warm sunshine rushing in through the open windows and the Pyrenees jutting out into the blue winter sky on the horizon. The Clarks came over in the evening and I like to remember never feeling so content. I was already looking forward to the next Christmas, with some amazing races to come in between.

My first assignment for 2001 was to be my favourite race of the whole of the previous year's calendar: the Jacob's Creek Tour Down Under. The team were once again ensconced in the wonderful Adelaide Hilton for the duration, whilst I was to be billeted in the Australian Institute of Sport's place on the sand at Henley Beach.

Unfortunately, it was not to be an idyllic stay.

The boys had arrived a week earlier than me, just after Christmas. Stevo was in charge, and he had Max, Ciaran, Tayeb, Mirko, John Tanner, Miguel Martin Perdiguero and Juan Carlos Dominguez with him, plus Craig, Richey and our new *soigneur* Ainhoa, a neighbour of Neil's from the Basque Country. Joining up in time for the off on the 16th would be Macca, Marcel Gono and Pete Rogers, directly after the Australian National Road Race.

Max was absolutely furious. Under his arrangement, his salary for 2000 was to have been paid in quite a complicated way: a normal wage of around £25,000 was to be paid monthly, like the rest of us, while the remaining £175,000 was to arrive in three drops through the year. As of January 2001, Max claimed not to have seen a single penny of the three big lumps. Eventually Max said that enough was enough and he was going to call a press conference and spill the beans in Australia.

This was also a major headache for Stevo, as he had to calm Max down and get the floundering team morale up despite having his own personal money issues. Hein Verbruggen, the president of the UCI, was in Adelaide as a guest of honour for the race, and Max wanted to have it out with him. Neil convinced Max that this was neither the time nor the place, and the big rendezvous waiting for us in a week's time in England was the arena to sort everything out.

Stevo was now having serious reservations about the whole set-up. He had agreed a deal with Xavier Mingez, the director of the recently defunct Vitalicio Seguros team, to buy one of their big team coaches, but the cash was not forthcoming. At a meeting in Cornebarrieu shortly before Christmas, Neil and Sean had sat down with Julian to discuss all issues such as these. Sean remembers Julian ranting on the phone to a finance man at McCartney's MPL, apparently trying to persuade MPL to release a payment for £270,000 to cover the mounting outgoings.

In Spain, Mingez was adamant to Stevo that his bank manager was telling him that there was no money arriving from England, and not to do anything with the coach (which we were desperate to get liveried in new McCartney/Jacob's Creek/Jaguar colours) until the money was safely in the Vitalicio account.

Neil had left for Australia with a simmering temper, promises and assurances ringing in his ears. His plan was to forget all the messy business for the duration of the race, ride for some good early season results, then return to England for the team launch immediately after Down Under and get some serious talking and ultimatums met there.

I emailed Julian to warn him of the current running through the team:

> Stevo has had to calm Max down again this morning. Max bumped into Hein Verbruggen in the foyer this morning – Max didn't say anything, but he told Stevo that he was going to ring Alain Rumpf today. I think that Stevo has seen off this particular problem, but the situation remains pretty volatile. Obviously, with Verbruggen in town, the temptation is there for any disgruntled rider . . .

He replied,

> I have just sent Neil and Max a long email regarding the situation. Although I appreciate it has been a bad situation to be part of, remember that it is me that runs this team.

There were more problems ahead. I was desperate to get a press release out regarding the Jaguar deal, as the guys were by now out training in their lovely new strip and would be racing in it in just a couple of days. It was such a good story that I was sure I could get some decent daily news coverage back home, especially as mid-January is not the best time for sport and there is often space to fill. Several papers were interested in running a piece about the team and its prestigious new sponsors, whose identity I had been teasing them about.

With time running out before the first stage of the Tour Down Under, I pressured Julian into giving me the green light for the press release. The hold-ups were put down to Jaguar's main man in the deal, Colin Cook, being away in Detroit and uncontactable. Finally, I got the go-ahead from Julian on 16 January, the day that the Tour Down Under was to start with a short evening circuit race in the Adelaide seaside resort of Glenelg.

Despite the friction and difficulties of the fraught preceding week, the team put up an excellent performance in Glenelg. It was a beautiful warm evening, the sun setting as the riders finished the 25 short laps of the town, and our big 2001 season under way. After Cello Gono, Macca and Ciaran had stretched the *peloton* with some serious pace over the last few laps, Ciaran had enough of a kick to take fourth place behind local boy Graeme Brown, while Macca was seventh. 'I'm well pleased with fourth today,' said Ciaran. 'Guys like Graeme Brown have been riding these races flat out since Christmas; I've been in Ireland and France and haven't raced since October. A couple more days like this and I'll have some sprinting speed in my legs.'

There was a worrying surprise waiting for me back at the pressroom. I logged on to sift through the daily emails to find one from a lady called Jill Wyatt at Jaguar. It read:

> John
> I understand there is a story in today's press that Jaguar is sponsoring the Linda McCartney team. It has been made very clear to Julian Clark by my colleague, Amanda Chick, that we are

not sponsoring the Linda McCartney team and that they cannot use our logo without permission.

I would be very pleased if you could email me by return with an explanation as to how this information has been released. We are now starting to get enquiries from newspapers about this sponsorship deal.

Kind regards

Jill

Due to the frustrations of time difference between Adelaide and Europe, I could not ring Jill, her colleague Colin Cook or Julian. I forwarded the message to Julian, who replied with a reassuring email:

Hi John,

Yes I have been dealing with Colin Cook today.

Although this has been agreed now you have seen this in December after we dealt with the situation with the Stevo thing they did not want to be part of it.

The agreement is there and it will be pushed more through France and Italy.

I know the situation is fragile there but do not add to it with this negativity. This has been discussed between me and LMC foods and has been something I have been dealing with for over a month.

For your info I now have a meeting with Paul and Mary to discuss things with the team as well as things are not gelling with Heinz, i.e. being told that we have too strong a vegetarian image and they want to come away from that and only be seen to push healthy eating.

Colin Cook will be making his own statement re the team.

Cheers

Julian

What did he mean? The Stevo thing? They didn't want to sponsor us because of that? Or they did, but were going to do it in France and Spain? And if that was the case, why did he give the go-ahead for the team strip to be made and the press release to go out? And what was this stuff about Heinz?

I spoke to Julian on the phone later that day, when he reiterated his intention to arrive in Australia before the end of the race to straighten everything out. The Jaguar thing was nothing to worry about: the sponsorship deal had been done through a different department, which is why Jill had sent that email. He was annoyed that I'd sent it before she had been informed, but agreed that it was necessary to have the news out before the racing started. Heinz were apparently not interested in using the team because our image was 'too vegetarian'. Julian was taking the problem straight to Paul McCartney to get it solved.

I was finding things a bit tricky in Adelaide. The atmosphere under Stevo was very different to that with Sean. For starters, I was staying out on the coast at Henley Beach as in 2000, when I had all the Australian teams in the race for company. This year, I found myself the AIS's only resident, as all the teams in the race were in the Hilton this time round. Driving downtown for breakfast with the boys had been a fixture of last year's race, and indeed we had always all eaten together throughout the year, but the first morning I did that in Australia, I was in for a nasty surprise.

'What are you doing here?' asked Neil as I sat down with a bowl of cereal. 'You're the press officer, not a rider. I don't expect to see you here unless it's on business, OK?' I sloped off a little downcast to the pressroom, but things were not destined to get any better. One of the features of our immensely popular team website had always been some not-too-serious pen pictures of the backroom staff written by me. For instance, Sean's one went, 'Every rider lives with a deep-seated fear of hearing Sean speak those fateful words: "I'll come out for a spin with you tomorrow." Still heard to criticise wheels for being "a bit flexy when you get out of the saddle uphill in the 12 sprocket". Ugly varicose veins approaching epidemic proportions, and will surely induce eventual halt of lifelong leg shaving. Moments of brilliant perception and comedy intersperse general illiteracy. Puts his weirder traits down to experimental schooling.' In a similar vein, Julian 'insists on using his useless French when drunk', and Cel was 'the sort of man who calls a spade a fucking shovel'. Craig was described as cycling's worst name-dropper, while our website genius Stuart Howell became a bedridden anorak.

These had always been a popular feature, so I wrote new ones for Stevo, Richey, Ainhoa and Arnaud. The new DS got another ribbing over his hair. This time he was 'owner of the most renowned haircut in world sport, but the king mullet that was once capable of winning races in its own right takes a back seat these days'. To accompany it, Stuart found a fantastic picture of a NASCAR type with a blond mullet and Oakleys who bore a striking resemblance to our man on the esteemed website, www.mulletsgalore.com.

Well, you can guess the next bit. He was absolutely not amused. 'Hey, Neil, check out my new addition to the website,' I suggested when he visited the pressroom. He stood staring at the screen for a few moments before I ventured a tentative, 'What do you think?'

'Pretty average,' he said. 'We're trying to build a professional outfit like Mapei or Once here. This kind of thing is no help at all.'

I had it taken down. I have to say that I totally disagreed with the Legend on this point: people liked us precisely because we *weren't* like Mapei or Once. We were different, a breath of fresh air, and a reminder that you don't have to be boring. The fact that there had been a hard core of us involved since we had been a small British domestic team had also helped to create that team spirit and individual image – the vegetarian thing had also brought us closer together, and marked us out as different; proudly different. I think Neil underestimated the usefulness of that attitude. He was determined to build a totally new team completely in the image of Saiz's Once – a worthy model for a brand new team, but difficult to reconcile to an already established outfit. There was more to come.

The team messed up on Stage Two. Week-long stage races like the

Tour Down Under are usually decided by seconds, and the die is often cast on the first proper stage. If a break gathers much time, the race is effectively over for all those teams who miss out – that's what had happened here a year previously, when Matt Stephens had gone with a move right near the beginning of the first long road stage and ended up in the top ten on the day and eventually overall. Well, that break went again, and we missed it.

There was a bit of bad luck involved, as Ciaran, Dominguez and John Tanner all made the first selection of the day. Unfortunately, they weren't really the right guys to have in there. John was in his first big race for us after a season of purely domestic British races, while Ciaran and Juan Carlos were at a relatively early point in their condition, with their main targets set in May. We would have been much better advised to have slotted Macca or Cello in there, as the Australian season was in full flow, and those guys were effectively our main men for this week.

The mistake was borne out a little later, as O'Grady attacked the break and split it again. The three McCartney men were in the wrong part of the resulting split, losing the best part of four minutes to O'Grady, Sacchi and Nardello's group by the time they reached the finish in Murray Bridge. Game over as far as the overall race was concerned; stage victories would now be our only aim in a race that we had hoped to contest. Stevo was furious, but his real anger would not be manifested until the next day.

On the third stage, Fabio Sacchi's Saeco teammate Andrea Galletti took off on a courageous day-long solo break. It was a hot South Australian day, and the bunch were generally happy to let him get on with it while the favourites from yesterday's break kept their beady eyes on each other. Galletti built up a lead of around 20 minutes that was certain to win him the stage, although it was likely to be whittled away in the closing stages. It was when the attack reached its biggest time gap that Stevo delivered a surprising instruction via the two-way radio that connected him to the riders: attack.

It was hot. The day was lost. There was nothing to gain. Nobody attacked.

'Why didn't you attack?' Neil demanded at the finish.

'Attack?' asked Dave incredulously. 'I thought you were joking.'

'OK, you're riding home.'

'Oh, come on, boss, you're not serious,' said Cello.

'You're riding home too,' he was told.

'I am taking the first plane home,' said a thoroughly pissed-off Tayeb.

'You'll be riding to it then,' said Stevo.

And so we ended up with half the team riding the 90 km back to Adelaide after racing 165 km under the Australian summer sun, and all this in January. Things were certainly going to be different under Neil Stephens – he was determined to make his mark early.

Stevo's vehemence brought impressive results. The following day's stage was the hottest of all, the temperature touching 45 centigrade in the hicksy town of Strathalbyn hosting the finish, but Linda McCartney riders were constantly active. Dave McKenzie was always involved, his animation bringing him the reward of the black jersey given to the day's 'Most Aggressive Rider', but it was Marcel Gono who so nearly took the team's first win of 2001. His counter-attacking group hit the front of the race just as Macca's move was recaptured virtually in sight of the line, and he threw everything into opening up the sprint early. 'A guy tried to jump just before the last corner, so I went under him on the turn and went all-out for the line,' said Marcel. 'Maybe it was a bit far, say 300 metres, and Luke Roberts came round me in the last two or three feet.'

Ciaran and Tayeb also made the top ten, diffusing some of the smoke that had been pouring out of their manager's ears 24 hours earlier.

Pete Rogers was staying with the team and riding the race, but in the jersey of the composite Mitsubishi-Sun Smart team of Australians put together just for the race. He was within a whisker of victory on the following day's penultimate stage, when he was pipped by Telekom's experienced Kai Hundertmark on the line in Tanunda only by the German's well-timed lunge.

Within a day, we would be celebrating the first win of the year.

Macca's solo victory in Adelaide was a masterpiece of intelligent, powerful riding, using his skill and knowledge to open up the opportunity, then making the most of his great power and form to press home the advantage. Very briefly, things were looking up again.

Chapter 11: Sean Yates's Lonely Hearts Club Band

Celebrations on Sunday night had been muted. Everybody relaxed with a glass of Jacob's Creek at the now traditional post-Tour Down Under beano, but nobody was in the mood for partying till dawn, unlike many of the European pros who blundered bleary-eyed back into the Hilton at 5 a.m. Tension had been apparent all week, as many McCartney riders and staff were still seeking payment for their services in 2000. Some had been paid up to date, some were owed a couple of months, some were owed more, some were paying for the team's expenses out of their own pockets, as the company credit card seemed to have packed up. The tension was heightened by the non-appearance in Australia of Julian Clark. He had been expected to visit the race to welcome Jacob's Creek to the team in their own backyard, and the boys were all very keen to discuss their problems with him.

Sciandri had been particularly vociferous. 'I don't want to hear any more of "the cheque's in the post", or "bank transfers take a few days", or "it'll be in your account tomorrow", I just want my money so I can ride my bike,' he explained.

His new manager, Neil Stephens, also unpaid since the back end of 2000, managed to convince Max that holding a press conference in Adelaide to air his concerns was not the best way of dealing with things. 'Once we get back to England, everybody will be there, and we can get it all sorted,' reasoned the Australian.

So we find ourselves at sticky Adelaide airport, winging our way back to London for Thursday's official photocall and Friday's team launch in Trafalgar Square. The race organisation has paid for the team to fly business class on Malaysian Airlines; unfortunately, that doesn't include Pete Rogers and me. The team pays for my ticket, so I'm happy to be in economy. Team rules dictate that before the season starts, it is the rider's own responsibility to get himself to his new home, so Pete has scraped together enough funds to pay for his own passage.

Pete stretches his long legs out across the space in front of us – we've landed the sought-after seats by the door – and we chew the fat about the season stretching in front of us. I tell Pete how much he's going to enjoy living in Toulouse, riding in the Midi–Pyrenees, meeting all the new friends that we've made. He says he's looking forward to his programme mapped out by Sean Yates and Neil Stephens, building steadily towards his first Giro d'Italia in May. I make a note to order him the Shimano shoes he needs when we get to Toulouse on Saturday, where we've got tickets for Toulouse FC v. Monaco, the big relegation showdown.

The seats are reclined and we drift off to sleep.

When we arrive in London on Tuesday, 23 January, the sort of chaos reserved, it seems, solely for cycling teams awaits us at Heathrow. Richey Wooles, our dependable new *soigneur*, is counting the various pieces of luggage on the 10 or 12 trolleys we're hogging, and we reckon we're missing at least 12 bits. Most of those missing will probably be large nylon black bags with 'Linda McCartney Pro Cycling Team' on the side and three-grand worth of Principia inside. That perennial nightmare of looking out of a 747 window in Kuala Lumpur in a few weeks' time and seeing some local peasants riding around the asphalt on a bike saying 'Juan Carlos Dominguez' along the top-tube comes back to haunt me. The joys of international bike racing.

By the time we get to The Cricketers Hotel in Bagshot, Max and Sean have already left for talks with Tim Treharne, MD of Linda McCartney Foods. Tim has been involved with the team since its very inception, as it was his desk that Julian Clark's proposal for a cycling team landed on back at the start of 1998. Max and Sean are concerned that they still haven't been paid, and they want to see how much Tim knows about the situation.

When they get back, they've got some pretty shocking news for us. It appears that despite the name emblazoned across our new strip, and the press release that I sent out on 16 January, Jaguar were not sponsoring the team in 2001. It appeared that negotiations had not progressed beyond an early stage, and their subsequent inclusion on the jersey and in all our plans would remain an ongoing mystery.

Not unreasonably, people began asking me what it was all about. Surely I must have known that all was not well with the Jaguar deal? A dull sick feeling began to grow in my stomach as I went over what I knew of the arrangement. I had written our original proposal to Jaguar back in July after Julian had made contact with Colin Cook, an executive of theirs. When Julian and I travelled down to San Sebastian to discuss the new strip with the manufacturers, Etxe-Ondo, in November, he'd told me the deal was as good as done, and that Etxe-Ondo would be incorporating it into the new design. We hadn't announced the arrangement before Christmas, as we were heralding Jacob's Creek's arrival, and didn't want the news to get lost in that excitement. And so, I'd written the joyful press release whilst in London for New Year's celebrations.

I didn't send it out then, though. First Julian explained that Jaguar were launching their F1 car, and wanted to delay until the following week, then Colin Cook was on holiday, then he was in Detroit on business. With the start of the Tour Down Under pressing, and our big press launch in Trafalgar Square just around the corner, we were under pressure to get the news out. On the 15th, Julian emailed me in Adelaide and said to send it out late the next day.

I was a bit concerned when an email arrived from a lady called Jill Wyatt at Jaguar, saying she had seen stories in the press about this new arrangement, and was at great pains to point out that there was no such agreement in place. We went to our rooms puzzled and heavy of heart, hoping that Julian would arrive in the morning and tell us that it was all part of some grand plan. Ever since I had met up with the guys in Australia, I thought that it was just a question of everybody getting paid. I was still confident that we would come up with the money, and the whole thing would be left behind us.

It was a sombre mood on the morning of Wednesday, 24 January, and Max called a meeting after breakfast. All of us: eighteen riders, three managers, three *soigneurs*, two mechanics, one doctor and one press officer; gathered in a little conservatory behind The Cricketers' restaurant to hear Max speak. There was silence in the room as he began to talk in his soft, easy accent. The Spanish guys huddled close to Stevo as he whispered a translation of Max's thoughts for them.

'OK, guys, this is the situation. Sean and I have spoken to Tim Treharne, and from what we can understand, the team has a lot of debts from last year, and the money that was expected from Jaguar isn't going to come. Julian seems to have promised us all certain things that he's not able to give us.

'I think it's time for us to move on and make a fresh start. Julian's tried everything he can, but now it's time for someone else to have a go. Now, I'm getting towards the end of my career, and I've been considering what to do with my future. I think we've got a great bunch of us together, and it would be terrible for us to break up. I guess, what I'm saying is, if you're all behind me, and you all want to do this, I'm prepared to take on the running of this team.'

Various questions were asked and answered: will Linda McCartney Foods make up the shortfall in budget? Maybe. Will it mean a wage cut? Possibly. Will we be doing the launch? Not yet. Will we be going to the Tour of Langkawi? No.

We'd talked in and out and around the subject for a few minutes before Sean suggested a vote on all going forward under Max's leadership. Tayeb nervously raised his hand and quietly asked, 'What if one of us already has an offer from another team?' There was a murmur of support round the room, everybody felt that if somebody had a chance to leave and could take it then the rest of us would wish him well, and support him in his choice. So with that proviso, the new regime was put to the vote. Max's new team got a unanimous welcome.

However, a few minutes later, supposedly shortly before everybody was going to go on a training ride, the sight of a couple of dozen guys in small huddles or talking on mobiles in different corners of the cold, damp car park told a different story.

SEAN YATES'S LONELY HEARTS CLUB BAND

I found myself in one of the small groups of frowning men shuffling from one foot to the other with hands in pockets, this one containing Sean, Chris Lillywhite and me. Chris was particularly worried. He'd used his own credit card to pay for the hire of two minibuses, a truck and the whole team's hotel bill. Sean was preparing to go back over to Tim Treharne's office in East Grinstead with Max, in an effort to thrash out a rescue plan.

It must have been at around this time when we were hit by the biggest bombshell yet. Sean turned back to Chris and me after taking a call on his mobile, his face betraying the tension and disappointment of an unwelcome piece of news.

'That was Tim,' he said. 'He's just received a fax from Julian, saying that the deal with Jacob's Creek had fallen through.'

We'd all believed that Jacob's Creek would be funding us to the tune of £1,700,000. Now we were staring down both barrels.

Max and Sean spent all day in East Grinstead, as the rest of us listlessly hung around, not knowing what to do with ourselves. The Spaniards, having reiterated their support for a rescue bid, flew home in the afternoon to await news and chase new prospective employers. By the time Sean and Max returned it was late, and journalists had started to gather. I felt some empathy with them; you could see they were excited about a big story unfolding, but sad that it was going to mean difficult times for the sport, and touched by the human plight of all the riders and staff.

The survivors squashed into the hotel lobby to hear how the afternoon had gone. Sean Yates has had critics over his time with the team, people complaining that he was inarticulate, brooding, even suggesting that he might not be the sharpest tool in the box. I wish those people could have been there to hear Sean speak so eloquently and succinctly that evening.

'It's not good news. The Jaguar deal won't be happening, the Jacob's Creek sponsorship is still under negotiation, and not for the amounts that we had heard mentioned. To cap it all, Linda McCartney have not agreed to put any money into the team this year, they were merely letting us continue using the name to attract other sponsors. So in the space of a few hours, we have gone from looking at a debt from last year and a shortfall for 2001, to literally no money at all. Tim is meeting with Nick Blair of Jacob's Creek tomorrow night to see if there's anything they can do, but otherwise it looks like the game is up. Julian collapsed on the plane over here and has been taken to hospital or something.

'Julian's been unsuccessful, but we need to remind ourselves about how persuasive and how enthusiastic he was. It's not just us who have bought into his plans, it's bank managers, investors, and managing directors of international companies. He convinced everybody.'

But there's the rub: he *nearly* convinced everybody. If he had convinced a couple more people, I wouldn't be writing this book. The team would have gone on to Mallorca for our first European race of the season, plans would have stepped up for the Giro and the Vuelta, schemes to see us to the start of the 2002 Tour would be under way and everybody would be feting Julian Clark as the hero of British cycling. It's a thin line.

According to Sean, he felt that if we had been talking about the sort of shortfall in budget that had looked likely that morning, McCartney may well have decided to back us and make up the difference. However, as the whole sorry story unravelled, Tim had left the room to call Paul McCartney.

He came back in and said, 'I've just spoken to Paul. He says "Walk away and call it a day, Tim," so I guess there's not much more we can do.'

Did Tim really call Paul McCartney? Who knows. Things we heard subsequently pointed to McCartney having already bailed the team out before, and he was hardly likely to do it again. Let me explain. We heard a rumour (I really do not know how true it was) that the budget for 2001 had run out shortly after the Giro. This would make sense, as it was around this time that cheques first began to go unpaid. Julian was perhaps banking on our Giro success leading to more coming in and the fabled Heinz investment was always expected, although it never arrived. Julian claims that Tim promised him at the finish of the Giro in Milan that Heinz had agreed to take over the budget and the McCartney investment from 2001 on. This would have given him good reason to push ahead with his plans for expansion – he would have been able to fund the basis of the team with the Heinz cash, and use new deals like the prospective Jacob's Creek and Jaguar contracts to pay for the increased salaries and staff numbers. But first there was the pressing issue of 2000 to see out with no money. The rumour had it that Paul McCartney forwarded the team's 2001 budget in the middle of 2000 in order to see out the season, and on the understanding that the Linda McCartney name was all he would get for 2001. That, and the standing of our team, would be all that would be necessary to bring in the extra sponsorship needed. It was a risky game, but we had taken risks since day one.

In light of this story, it would hardly seem likely that McCartney would bail us out again. I had heard a telling story from somebody in McCartney's MPL organisation soon after I joined the team: Paul had signed off a cheque for £57,000,000 to buy the rights to The Beatles' songs when the copyright was up on them, but the same day also refused to pay a £75 bill for having a gate fixed on his farm, on the grounds that he was being overcharged. Maybe this story is just one of the many myths that have grown up around McCartney, but if it is true, I think it shows that he is not 'tight', as some have rather predictably suggested over the years, but merely fears being made a fool of just because he is rich. He, and surely the vast majority of other people in his position, has enough money to do anything he wants, but he doesn't want people taking the piss out of him just because he is minted. Fair enough, I say.

That evening won't be forgotten in a hurry. As we sat in the bar, some pointedly ordering hamburgers, the gallows humour started to kick in. It was noted that Pete Rogers had managed to be in a team that had folded for each of the three previous years. He was landed with the extremely adhesive nickname of 'Jonah'. Then God in his wisdom decided that 'Penny Lane' would come loud and clear over the piped music system.

'Shut up!' somebody shouted, to some wry grins.

I took Tayeb to Stansted the following morning, Thursday, 25 January. He had a meeting with his manager where he hoped to tie up a deal with Lotto.

Then I ran Marlon Perez and Pete Rogers to Heathrow. Poor Jonah – he had paid for his own flight all the way here, it was to be his big break at last . . . and all for nothing. And Marlon – he had endured a four-hour strip search when he landed at Heathrow from Colombia on Tuesday; for what?

Most of the others ebbed away through the morning. Then Matt and I confirmed our membership of the '30 Somethings Mum's Club' as we both relied on our loving mothers to carry us away from the scene of the crime.

Last goodbyes said, final handshakes shook, it came to an end.

I couldn't help thinking about Julian. I knew him better than anybody, had shared an office with him for over a year, thought myself to be his right-hand man. How could I not have known the extent of our problems? He may have let people down, but I couldn't believe that he had done it maliciously, or for personal gain. I think he is simply the most energetic, ambitious person I've ever met, and he was prepared to do or say anything to try and realise the Tour de France dream of the Linda McCartney Pro Cycling Team. We shouldn't be too hard on him – after all, none of us would have been there at all if it hadn't been for his idea in the first place.

It was an exciting ride. We just weren't expecting it to stop so soon.

More stuff leaked out over the coming weeks. Richey and I flew back to Toulouse to get our stuff and move out of Aussonne. The *service course* was completely empty. We were told that the Spanish mechanics and *soigneurs* had cleared it out, and we guessed that someone else had removed anything they had left. For instance, my huge pile of press cuttings was gone: I don't know what a mechanic would have done with that. At my house, I welled up inside, choked that I would be leaving it for the last time, and so unexpectedly. I went into my garage to get the bike that Julian had given me for good service last year to find it stripped down to the bare frame and forks. Richey was told later that they had not had enough Shimano equipment to build the bikes due to be sent to Langkawi, so the mechanics had come round to my house to take the gear I had on my bike. The day before, I diligently collected the bikes that had arrived late at Heathrow from Adelaide and passed them on to the riders they were intended for. With hindsight, I guess I should have kept one, but I still hoped that somehow we were going to find a way out and still be the happy little team we had been for so long.

Tracie and Julian were still there at the house in Aussonne with Julian's mum when I called on them. I thought it only right that I should see them before leaving, to let them know that I still considered them to be friends, and always would.

Julian still felt that if he could get through to Paul McCartney directly and tell him his side of the story, he could rescue the situation. He wrote a letter to McCartney, and sent me a copy. This is it:

Dear Paul,

I understand Tim Treharne has been in touch with you over the last couple of days. I would like if I may the opportunity to get my situation across. Although I accept some of the responsibility for the outcome of the team I do not accept all.

In May of last year at the Tour of Italy, Tim Treharne flew out to the last stage of the race in Milan (the first time any representative from the company has come along) but only as our problems had already begun then.

That night I was told that he had been in contact with Heinz and they would be getting involved in the team and our financial shortfall would be over. Over the next seven months we built £180,000 overdraft up with our bank in the UK, £60,000 with the bank in France, £28,000 to the VAT, plus £140,000 in other loans from people and family just to keep the team alive. There is also arrears in the team with wages and expenses totalling £3,000. One example: one of the members in the team who also was a good friend used his own credit card to pay the hotel bill while the team were in the UK this week. He is now out of pocket. I have not paid myself for six months. We now have to face bankruptcy and next week when I go back to France we are forced to sell our house to pay that bank. All this without the fact of losing something which we had a huge belief in and thought was our future. I have a wife, a boy of six and one of 20 months, you may remember she was pregnant at the same time as Mary when we came to your recording studio with the team.

I have been staying with a doctor friend of my parents for the last two days with total exhaustion. For the riders in the team that have any salaries still to come I instructed them today to sell our team lorry and divide the money up.

I am sure you have a lot on your plate and don't see much about the team but I would like you to know that across mainland Europe the team has been getting front-page coverage, and if you had seen the millions of roadside spectators in Italy at the Tour Italy, shouting 'Linda, Linda, Linda', and 'Forza Vegetarianos', I believe you would have been over the moon.

I believe it is Heinz that should have been investing in the team and using it as a vehicle to promote the foods, but only last week I was told by a representative from them that they would not be investing in the team as it had built too strong a vegetarian image and this was not what they wanted. They needed to go the healthy living route.

I have driven this team with the image that both yourself and Linda had wanted relentlessly and had got it to a position where it had proved the doubters wrong that this was not possible.

When David McKenzie won that stage of the Tour of Italy, at the finish there were over 350,000 spectators and it was on TV in 120 countries. In Australia last week at the Tour Down Under we won again and the team were all over the papers and invited onto breakfast TV shows to talk about the foods and the lifestyle. This we get in every country we go to.

> I know it probably is not possible but I would really like the
> opportunity to meet with you and talk face to face about this. I
> am until the weekend staying in Tunbridge Wells.
>
> Kind Regards
> Julian Clark

Sean set about recovering the riders' lost wages from 2000 through the
UCI, as every team has to lodge a bond of three months' salary for each
employee before they are allowed to race. There was already a furore
about the 2001 bond, as it naturally had not been paid, yet we were
allowed to compete in Australia.

There were complications getting any cash out of the UCI. They
claimed that the necessary bank documents were not up to scratch, and
no bond had been paid in 2000. Julian refuted this. There had, I
remembered, been a great deal of to-ing and fro-ing at the start of 2000
regarding the bond. Julian says that he suggested lots of different ways of
paying the bond, all of which were rejected or ignored by the notoriously
red-tape-riddled UCI. Eventually, he says he sent them a specimen bank
draft, saying, 'What if I do it like this?' He didn't hear from them
regarding the matter again, so decided not to pursue it. They now told
us that the document Julian said was a 'specimen' had been interpreted
as the real thing – and of course, the money didn't exist.

Sean and everybody else owed money were furious. The UCI were
supposed to protect us: now they were not only telling us that we weren't
covered for 2001, we had raced all year in 2000 with no bond in place –
they were passing the buck. Daniel Malbranque of the CPA, the riders'
union, took up our case. He argued that the UCI were responsible for
meeting the bond as they had accepted it as genuine whether it was or
not, and it had been their responsibility to check its veracity.

Eventually, we got some cash. I got one month's money, which was less
than what I was owed, but as I had written it off I was happy.

I saw Julian one more time. I went back to France at Easter to see some
friends and pick up some more stuff. It would have been easier not to,

but I felt I should go round there. We had a chat and a cup of coffee. He was doing some landscape gardening and waiting for the sale of our truck to go through so that he could pay off all the creditors. I don't know what became of that plan.

'John, you know I'm sorry about what happened,' he said as we walked back to the garden gate.

'That's OK,' I replied, pretty weakly. I didn't know what else to say.

'Listen, I'm on the verge of setting up a new team. Cel's going to be the DS, and I've got a load of cheap eastern Europeans lined up to ride. The title sponsor is going to be a meat company – like the twist? "Meat company put life back into vegetarian team," something like that? They're just waiting for this foot and mouth thing to blow over in Britain. Do you want to be involved?'

Even then, after everything, I couldn't just say no. He was so enthusiastic, so into it.

'I think I'd have to think about it, mate,' I replied. That's the last time I saw him.

Epilogue

Late tonight I stand outside the house, the short grass cool and damp between my toes, but the earth beneath it hard and warm. My eyes warm to the night, slowly beginning to sense stars behind the stars. The Milky Way, so clumsily yet beautifully named, a long dull smudge that can only be seen properly when you look away. Planes with fizzing lights slide across an invisible glass table-top way above like pebbles on an icy pond. Silent until they pass, they seem to be hurtling as if fired from a distant gun and no longer powered at all . . . but then, in their wake, the roar of their far-off engines emerges to chase them onwards to who knows where.

The house, lights on and curtains open, stares out into the gloom hopefully yet blindly. With its two bay windows for eyes, it can serve no purpose other than to disturb the dark and make the night harder to feel. With the eyes shut, lights extinguished, the dark is all around, comforting and unthreatening, the warmth of the bricks at my back reassuring to the last.

From the east a chattering low roar begins as the late Portsmouth Harbour train spans the forest between Liphook and here, the lights from inside the spartan carriages briefly flickering behind the trees. The dim yellow glow falls momentarily on to the passing fields, giving them the tint of a silent movie. For a second a bat is captured in the light, frozen as if in a silent film, the imprint of his flitting image remaining long after the tiny wings have carried him away.

An owl hoots. Voices carry faltering on the air from a garden three or four fields distant, as the last drops are squeezed from the last bottle of red before bed.

Suddenly, a pinprick of light scrapes the night at unimaginable speed and is gone, its path etched on the sky, or perhaps just on my eye. I close both of them very tightly, the shooting star still burning a picture through my closed eyelids, and I wish for something. I wish for it as hard as one can wish before the wish becomes a prayer. A wish that hard must be heard somewhere in the night.

Appendix: Where Are They Now?

TAYEB BRAIKIA
Well looked after by his manager Henrik Elmgreen, Tayeb moved fairly seamlessly to Lotto, where he picked up a couple of the good wins that had eluded the fast-finisher during his year at McCartney. Victim of a horrific crash in Spain that could have claimed his life in the spring of 2001, Tayeb has sadly not been able to regain full race fitness and was forced to retire in early 2002. A talent unfulfilled.

BEN BROOKS
Ben has matured into an excellent, classy rider, currently plying his trade with Team Down Under, a collection of antipodeans riding low-budget races in Belgium. 'It's weird to go from being the baby of the team to the most experienced inside of a year,' he laughs. A couple of big results should bring him the pro-contract his class deserves.

MATT DE CANIO
Matt picked up a ride with the US-based Saturn team, much improved from his time at McCartney. Benefited from being released before the end of 2000, thus leaving himself with more team options for 2001.

JULIAN CLARK
Believed to be back living in Kent after a spell in Her Majesty's custody over charges dating back to the Brands Hatch gym days. Now working in landscape gardening . . . but the next big idea must surely be fermenting.

INIGO CUESTA
The instantly recognisable figure of Cuesta, stocky, cap on back to front, chubby cheeks under the permanent Oakleys is a constant presence in the front group of all the big tours. Cofidis benefited greatly from the McCartney team's demise by signing such a reliable lieutenant for David Millar.

JOHN DEERING
Trundling in from his Sussex–Hampshire country mansion (so big it's in two counties) to Kingston-Upon-Thames every morning, just like the old days. Still pushing the Principia round the North Downs on Sunday mornings, if not travelling to another glamorous location with the Sigma Sport team. Incredibly popular with the ladies, naturally.

KIT DEERING
Living in domesticated splendour with her mistress in Leicestershire, she may have lost a little of her pace, but none of her energy. Bit wider around the middle these days, but that's what happens to chocolate Labradors. Still beautiful.

LOUISE DEERING
Successfully running her own company supplying staff to big distribution centres. Never seen without a mobile phone clamped to her ear. Briefly came out of retirement to *soigneur* for the Sigma Sport team at the 2002 Lincoln Grand Prix, but has no plans to get back into cycling on a more permanent basis.

JUAN CARLOS DOMINGUEZ
Rode out 2001 on a low wage with Banesto, but has come into his own as leader of the Swiss Phonak squad, winning the 2002 Giro d'Italia prologue and taking the leader's pink jersey in the process. Always a danger man in the one-week stage races.

CRAIG GEATER

Now beavering away at the crack Danish CSC-Tiscali squad for his second season. Craig has been an unqualified success, proving that good mechanics will always be sought after. There's not many of his calibre about.

SCOTT GUYTON

Riding in Belgium with the McKenzies' iTeamNova set-up after two years conquering the bergs for the Flanders team. Becoming more Flandrian every day . . . he won't be recognised back home.

MATT ILLINGWORTH

'I've become White Van Man. I love it.' Having moved into a flat within puking distance of his favourite pub in Leigh-on-Sea, all rumours of a comeback from the big feller are instantly squashed. We live in hope. Turned down a ride with Sigma Sport in 2002, explaining, 'If you give me a bike you might want me to ride it.'

ALLAN IACUONE

Rode for the Czech Wustenrot team in 2000, before retiring, disillusioned, halfway through the year. Coaxed out of it by the McKenzies to make a successful return to racing with iTeamNova, picking up an excellent win in Yugoslavia.

KEITH LAMBERT

Lego finds enough work at his shop and his catalogue bike supply business to keep him out of team management for the time being, which is good news for the rest of us trying to get teams winning races in the UK. Managers of his class and experience coming up against us we can well do without, thank you.

CHRIS LILLYWHITE

Cel has become a secret triathlete, training under cover of darkness and behind closed doors before unleashing his power on an unsuspecting tri-

hard public. Won his first two events. Has also managed to do something that eluded him throughout his pro career: broke his collarbone whilst doing 10 mph in Richmond Park, thus needing a metal plate to be fitted. Now a plumber of distinction.

DAVID McKENZIE
Set up iTeamNova with his wife Susan after a low-key year in Switzerland. The unique team is funded by individual sponsorships and contributions from fans. Overcame a nasty crash in the winter whilst training in Melbourne to return to Europe for the 2002 season. Super-motivated to achieve more success for their lovely baby girl, Lulu.

CHRIS NEWTON
Had an excellent 2000 and 2001, riding a fantastic Olympic team pursuit with Bradley in Sydney, then winning the Circuit de Mines stage race. Will be a top UK rider for years to come.

MAURIZIO DE PASQUALE
Exact whereabouts unknown, but believed to be retired and living in Italy. Probably running a magic mushroom farm or Ben & Jerry's outlet.

MIGUEL MARTIN PERDIGUERO
His second year in Italy is looking good, playing second fiddle in the sprints to Mario Cipollini at Aqua Sapone. Rode strongly alongside JCD at the 2002 Settimaine Catalonia, picking up a good stage win.

CIARAN POWER
Ciaran reluctantly left Toulouse at the end of 2001 after riding that year with the French St Quentin/Oktos outfit. He and Lisa were married in Waterford, and then left for the USA to take up his new role as a 'hitter' for Navigators. 2002 then saw him win his second Milk Ras Tour of Ireland. Still looking at a great future.

ROB REYNOLDS-JONES

Last heard muttering the immortal greeting, 'Skipton Electrical, can I help you?' The Log still prowls the hillsides of Bolton Abbey in his Silver Arrow: 'If you see it rocking, don't come knocking.'

PASCAL RICHARD

Fell out with, first, the McCartneys for failure to turn up at races, then with the Swiss Olympic selectors for failing to take him to Sydney despite his being the reigning champion. Retired in anger at the conclusion of the 2000 season, withdrawing his artefacts from the Swiss Olympic Museum display.

PETE ROGERS

Last heard of working in his brother's bike shop in Canberra. 'I got an offer to go to Switzerland with Macca, but I can't afford to ride for no money again,' he reasoned.

MARK SCANLON

Rode for the Irish national squad before accepting an offer to ride with the American Mercury team in 2002. Last seen by the author on the cobbled climbs of the 2001 Lincoln Grand Prix, where he remarked, 'I've got a feeling this is a better race to watch than it is to ride, John!'

MAX SCIANDRI

Max stepped into the breach at Lampre when their fragile superstar Franck Vandenbroucke couldn't cut it in 2001, giving his new sponsors one of the best spring campaigns of his career. They rewarded him with a two-year contract – not bad for a 35 year old. Still in great shape and always a force to be reckoned with.

SPENCER SMITH

Spencer has come into his own as an Ironman triathlete, excelling in the event where a 2.5-mile open water swim, 100-mile bike ride and marathon are de rigueur. Victories in Brazil and Florida have confirmed him as one of the best triathletes the world has ever seen. Like Matt, supported by Sigma Sport.

JOSH STEPHENS
The little feller that put his mum and dad through such trauma over the back end of 2000 is not such a little feller any more. Growing fast and learning quickly, will surely soon outpace his old man . . . just like the rest of us.

MATT STEPHENS
Returned to the UK to become leader of the Sigma Sport team. Winner of the Manx International in 2001. Qualified as a police officer in Cheshire in early 2002, whilst still remaining a feared competitor on the British race circuit.

HEIKO SZONN
Pops up unexpectedly from time to time anywhere within the Brisbane–Berlin–Sittingbourne triangle to impress any watching nyrons with an impressive show of strength before disappearing once more to whence he came . . . a laboratory high in the Carpathian Mountains, perhaps?

JOHN TANNER
Perennially the most impressive performer on home roads, John returned to the fold of his Pro Vision team to once again cane all British opposition during 2001. The team has strengthened into the Compensation Group line-up for 2002.

ADRIAN TIMMIS
Contracted by British Cycling to work with the GB mountain bike squad, Ada gets to travel to plenty of idyllic locations around the globe and put his feet up for a few days. Perfect. Now the owner of a Sports Science degree and one of the most sought-after masseurs in the country.

BJORNAR VESTOL

There will surely always be a place available for such a willing powerhouse as the Norwegian. He has spent the last two years at the quietly improving Danish Fakta squad.

CHRIS WALKER

Officially retired at the end of 2000 to become a wheeler-dealer. Still keen on becoming a fireman if he can learn to write well enough to pass the entrance exam. Lives in perpetual South Yorkshire bliss with Lynne, Jessie, Joey and Fidget.

EDDIE WEGELIUS

His early departure from Linda McCartney worked out well for Eddie: he is working for the Bonjour team where the professional set-up and surrounds suit him well. More experienced than when he joined us, he has become a very well respected *soigneur*.

BRADLEY WIGGINS

Brad went back on to the Performance Plan for a successful season with the GB team before landing a contract with Francaise des Jeux for 2002. Eased in gently for his first full European year, great things are expected in the future.

JULIAN WINN

Still chasing the title of Fastest Welshman, Winnie has confirmed himself as one of the most accomplished riders on the British circuit. It doesn't matter where the race is or what the course is like, he'll be somewhere near the front. Possibly the keenest trainer the cycling world has ever seen – there's not much else to do in Abergavenny. Became GB Road Race Champion in 2002.

RICHEY WOOLES

Went back to his previous employers, the GB World Class Performance Programme, and has been rewarded for his hard work by landing the prestigious post of Women's Endurance Coach. I expect their HQ is extremely tidy.

SEAN YATES
Enjoyed a year of labouring on various sites around the Home Counties before taking the plunge again with the DS post at iTeamNova. Seems a lot more relaxed second time around . . . does a career in top cycling management still beckon? I think it could.